EAT LIKE A LOCAL IN TURIN

BITE-SIZED FOODIE GUIDES

Gusto Publications

ISBN 979-1220014151

For permission requests, write to the publisher at anna@italywithgusto.com.

CONTENTS

INTRODUCTION

Despite its rich cultural heritage and delicious food, Turin is, certainly, one of the most underrated Italian cities. After the glorious days when the Savoy royal house resided here, Turin slowly became a provincial, albeit affluent, backwater known for its FIAT car manufacturing and the Juventus Football Club. However, things changed after the 2006 Winter Olympic Games. The event put the city on the tourist map and helped to start its rejuvenation. Today, Turin welcomes over 4,000,000 tourists annually and The New York Times ranked it as one of the top 52 destinations for 2016.

Unique local and regional dishes, echoes of aristocratic France and neighbouring Liguria all contribute to Turin's distinctive cuisine. The city's grand historic cafes, charming centuries-old sweet shops, innovative chocolatiers, sumptuous delicatessens and lively markets make Turin a must-visit destination for foodies with something to satisfy the most refined palates. It has embraced the Slow Food movement that was born in Piedmont and has numerous slow fast food outlets that pride themselves in sourcing only local seasonal ingredients. The city's large multicultural population means that there are plenty of excellent ethnic restaurants and shops. Turin's recently elected mayor promotes a plant-based diet as part of the local government's political aims (unsurprisingly, to much grumbling by locals) making the city vegetarian-friendly.

I travel to eat. If you are holding this book, it is safe to assume that you are a foodie like me. Naturally, museums, art galleries and archaeological sites are high up on my agenda but rubbing shoulders with locals in a cosy bar or traditional restaurant while learning about the city's everyday life and eating like a local are certainly my priorities.

I don't just ask locals where to eat when I arrive to a new destination. I ask them what I should eat to understand the heart and soul of the city. Nothing tells you more about the place than a local traditional dish. It is like a history lesson on a plate. Anchovies in a green salsa remind you about strong trade connections that Turin had with Liguria; a hearty dish of slowly cooked cockscombs, organ meats and mushrooms flavoured with Marsala make you think of the poor peasants who came to sell their produce at the city's markets many centuries ago; delicious hazelnut chocolates remind you of the 19th-century naval blockade that put a strain on the local gourmands.

If you travel in search of special gastronomic experiences, Turin is the right place for you as it offers some extraordinary delights that you will remember long after leaving the city. Where else can you enjoy a chocolate-covered ice cream on a stick invented by a local family on a historic piazza, devour tiny lobster sandwiches served on a silver plate by a uniformed waiter or start your morning with a rich Cointreau-spiked hot chocolate? You will find all these, and more, only in Turin!
This culinary guide is different from many others. It is a

collection of interviews that I did with twelve Turin residents from different walks of life. They told me about their favourite local dishes and foods that, in their opinion, make the city's cuisine special, as well as when, how and where to eat them. They also shared their childhood memories and gastronomic tips. In this book, you will find 90 addresses of restaurants, bars, cafes, bakeries, chocolatiers, food and ice cream shops and markets that locals love, learn about 30 traditional dishes and foods, many of which can only be found in Turin, and get a glimpse of the city that normally remains hidden from tourists. How about summer lunch at a rowing club with stunning views over the River Po? Or brunch at a cosy literary club with red velvet chairs and gilded mirrors? Fancy having an early evening drink with gourmet snacks in a 19th-century pharmacy or a bijou perfume shop? You will read about these extraordinary places and many others in this book.

By no means is this book a comprehensive guide. It is an introduction that aims to tickle your curiosity and make you want to learn and taste traditional dishes that might be hard to find outside of Turin. Use it together with conventional travel guides to Turin to plan unforgettable meals and find unique gastronomic experiences.

THINGS TO REMEMBER

Opening hours may change depending on the season (e.g. some restaurants and bars stay open longer in summer). Although every effort has been made to ensure that correct opening hours are listed in the book, if you are planning a very special meal please call ahead to enquire and book a table.

Many shops and eateries are closed on Sunday and Monday afternoon. In August and some days prior to and after Christmas holidays, you might find some places shut for at least a week with a sign *"Chiuso per ferie"* ("Close for holidays") on the door.

You will be surprised how easy it is to navigate the city without speaking a word of Italian. Turin's large student population means that many restaurants, bars and cafés will have young staff members who speak at least some English.

In summer, many cafes and restaurants have outdoor tables (*dehors*). Be prepared for a slower service in busy periods if you are sitting outside. The lively atmosphere and, if you are on a beautiful piazza, the views are certainly worth the wait.

If you are heading for a meal in a small traditional style *piola* eatery, make sure you have cash as many of them do not accept credit cards.

Price range:

All restaurant listings in this book have euro symbols to indicate the price range for a main course.

€...........€ 5-10
€€........€ 11-19
€€€......€ 20-30

TOP GASTRONOMIC EXPERIENCES IN TURIN

1. Rub shoulders with locals in a *piola*, a small eatery where traditional inexpensive simple meals are served. (see page 67)

2. Drink il *bicerin*, a mix of chocolate, coffee and cream, invented in Turin, in one of the city's historic cafés. (see page 37)

3. Enjoy an *aperitivo* or *apericena* with locals. (see page 15)

4. Stock up on artisan chocolates made in Turin's historic shops. (see page 24)

5. Gorge on tiny *tramezzini* sandwiches served on silver plates in the historic Café Mulassano where they were invented. (see page 72)

6. Dip vegetable sticks in *bagna cauda*, a strong traditional warm dip made with butter, garlic, anchovies and oil. (see page 11)

7. Crunch *grissini* breadsticks before dinner or as a snack. (see page 18)

8. Have a glass of warm *zabaione*, a sweet thick beverage made with egg yolks, sugar, and Marsala wine, accompanied by a buttery croissant for breakfast. (see page 52)

9. Eat traditional dishes in a local's home at a social eating event. (see page 32)

10. Try a "slow burger" made with strictly local ingredients sourced from the farms near Turin. (see page 41)

01 TRADITIONAL APPETISERS, TURIN-STYLE APERITIF AND REGIONAL CUISINE

Ciao, we are Marco Baroetto Parisi and Paola Tartaglino. Marco is born in Turin and works as an information technology engineer. Paola has grown up in the hills near the city of Asti and moved to Turin to study at the university and today works as an art historian. Together we write a travel blog Carapau Costante (www.carapaucostante.it) and Paola also runs a design blog We Make A Pair (www.wemakeapair.com).

Favourite dishes: we both go crazy for *antipasti*. A traditional Piemontese meal can be made up of only *antipasti*, or appetisers: *vitello tonnato, tomini al verde, pomodori* or *uova ripiene, peperoni con bagna caoda*.

Vitello tonnato – cooked veal slices served cold as an appetiser with a creamy mayonnaise, tuna and anchovy sauce. Some restaurants serve *"vitello tonnato alla vecchia manera"*, or the old way, which means without mayonnaise. The sauce in this case is made with tuna, capers, anchovies, meat broth and boiled egg yolks.

Tomini al verde – white soft cheese often stored in oil. It comes in small round shapes flavoured with herbs and spices. The smaller rindless *tomini* are traditionally served as starters topped with a strong green sauce (*bagnet verd*) which is made with parsley, garlic, olive oil, vinegar, bread crumbs and anchovies.

Pomodori ripieni – stuffed tomatoes are served as a cold appetiser. Different types of fillings exist: cheese, tuna, *grissini* breadsticks mixed with onions, *"bagnet"* (a mix of anchovies, parsley, egg yolk, garlic and bread crumbs soaked in vinegar and olive oil).

Uova ripiene – stuffed boiled eggs, a traditional style appetiser.

Boiled eggs are shelled, cut in half and filled with tuna, cheese, anchovies or breadcrumbs.

Bagna caoda (or **Bagna cauda**) – a traditional rich dip made with butter, garlic, anchovies and olive, hazelnut or walnut oil. In some parts of Piedmont cream is also added. *Bagna caoda* is served warm with vegetables and bread that are dipped in it. Normally it is eaten in autumn and winter. It is said that Papa Francesco loves *bagna caoda* and enjoys it as a treat every time he visits Piedmont.

Why: We like the idea of a meal made of many different dishes that you can choose from. We normally eat them on weekends with our families as both our sets of parents are experts in the local cuisine. These dishes also remind us of a tradition that is slowly disappearing: *marenda sinoira*. It is a meal served late in the afternoon and is composed of cold cuts, cheese and traditional appetisers, something between an afternoon snack and dinner (see the sidebar "La marenda sinoira").

Where: All our favourite dishes can be found in traditional trattorias called "*piole*". We like going to Antiche Sere and Da Celso (for more see "Rub shoulders with locals" on page 67). Turin has always been a city of diverse cultures, so here you will find excellent restaurants serving regional Italian cuisine as well as ethnic food. We recommend **Trattoria Ala** for simple Tuscan dishes, **Rosso Piccante** for southern italian cuisine and **Kirkuk Cafè**, in the city centre, that serves delicious Kurdish and Middle Eastern food.

"LA MARENDA SINOIRA" ·········▶
In old days, in the province of Turin *"la marenda sinoira"* (or *"la merenda sinoira"*) referred to a traditional cold meal served several hours before dinner especially in the countryside among peasant families after a day of work in the fields. It included several dishes that varied in different areas and among families: cheese, salami, ham, marinated and fresh vegetables, boiled potatoes, slices of cold polenta and fruit. In summer, this traditional late afternoon snack was also common among noble families staying at their countryside villas . Some food historians say that

the modern tradition of late afternoon aperitif with snacks came from *"la marenda sinoira"*. Nowadays, some bars offer *"la marenda sinoira"* on certain days. For instance, **Cantina Torino** (see page 40) serves what they call *"la marenda sinoira"* that consists of nine small cold appetisers to accompany your drink on Friday and Saturday from 6pm at a price of 16 euros (excluding drinks). For a more traditional style *"la marenda sinoira"*, try **Caffe-Vini Emilio Ranzini** (see more in the sidebar "Rub shoulders with locals in a traditional piola" on page 67) in the centre, not far from Il Duomo. Be warned, it is always packed with locals!

LE ANTICHE SERE €€

Address: Via Cenischia, 9, 10139 Turin

Tel: 0039 011 385 4347

Opening hours:

Monday - Saturday 7.30pm- 12am.

Closed on Sunday.

A cosy *osteria* serves simple traditional dishes from Piedmont. Make sure to try their *vitello tonnato* and the signature dishes *stinco di maiale* (slowly cooked pork shank), *coniglio in vino bianco* (rabbit in white wine) and *zabaione al moscato* served with *meliga* biscuits. Booking in advance is recommended as it is always busy.

DA CELSO €

Address: Via Verzuolo, 40, 10139 Turin

Tel. 0039 011 4331202

Opening hours: Wednesday and Sunday 12pm -3pm

Thursday – Saturday, 8pm – 1am. Closed on Monday, Tuesday. (Opening hours vary depending on the season).

Old style family-run trattoria with an outdated yet charming interior. Excellent traditional dishes such as *pasta tajarin al ragù*, *antipasti Piemontesi*, dessert *il bònet*, artisan salami. Credit cards are not accepted.

Trattoria Ala € €

Address: Via Santa Giulia, 24, 10124 Turin.
Tel.: 0039 011 8174778.
Opening hours: Monday - Saturday 12pm -14.30, 7pm-10.30pm. Closed on Sunday. www.trattoria-ala.it
Centrally located, the trattoria has been serving simple Tuscan dishes since 1950. The menu features hearty fish soups, pasta, wild boar and horse steaks, grilled lamb. It gets busy and noisy on weekends.

Rosso Piccante €

Address: via Galliari 24/b, 10125 Turin.
Tel.: 0039 011 6599323. www.rossopiccanteincucina.it
Opening hours: Every day 7.30am-12pm.
A deli with a small restaurant selling and serving tipical products and dishes from Calabria, Basilicata, Apulia and Campania: fresh *burrata* cheese, buffalo *mozzarella*, spicy salami *'nduja*, pasta, grilled sausages and traditional desserts.

Kirkuk Cafè € €

Address: Via Carlo Alberto, 16b/18, 10123 Turin.
Tel.: 0039 011 530657.
Opening hours: Tuesday - Friday 12-3pm, 7pm - 12am, Monday and Saturday 7pm - 12am. Closed on Sunday. www.kirkukkaffe.com
A small cosy eatery that serves delicious kebab, hummus, falafel and delectable Middle Eastern desserts. Has many vegetarian dishes on the menu (for more see "Addresses for vegetarians and vegans" on page 43).

Tip from a local: for an informal dinner, try aperitivo torinese (Turin-style aperitif): you pay for a drink and also get snacks that are included in the price. The best areas to find bars that serve good Turin-style aperitif are the Quadrilatero romano and San Salvario. We recommend Lanificio San Salvatore and La Cuite (for more see "Apericena" on page 15).

LANIFICIO SAN SALVATORE

Address: Via Sant'Anselmo, 30, 10125 Turin
Opening hours: Monday - Saturday 6pm - 2am,
Sunday 11am - 3pm.
A lively bar in the San Salvario area with a good choice of cocktails (try their excellent Mojitos with a touch of ginger!) and abundant buffet in the evening. Live bands play a few times a week with music varying from punk rock to jazz. On Sundays, the bar serves brunch.

LA CUITE

Address: Via Giuseppe Baretti, 11, 10125 Turin
Opening hours: Monday - Thursday and Sunday 5pm - 2am,
Saturday 5pm – 3am.
Unlike in many other bars in the city, you have to pay separately for small tapas-style snacks (mini-burgers, grilled cheese etc.), as they are not included in the price of a drink. Offers a good choice of wines, regional and international. Gets very busy on weekends.

Favourite ice cream shops: We think that the best ice cream in the city is in the gelateria MOSA. Our favourite flavour is *pistacchio* and all their fruit *sorbetti* are good too.

MOSA GELATERIA

Address: Via Muriaglio, 1, 10141 Turin
Opening hours: Every day 11am – 12am

Fresh artisan ice cream is made every day in classic flavours as well as in very imaginative seasonal variations such as *panettone* (available only during Christmas period), *Moscato* wine etc. For 8 euros you can taste all available flavours!

Vitello tonnato

TURIN-STYLE APERITIVO AND APERICENA

Turin claims the title of the birthplace of the *aperitivo* tradition. In the late 18th century, a local distiller named Antonio Benedetto Carpano created vermouth, a fortified wine flavoured with herbs, which was sold in his shop in the beautiful Piazza Castello accompanied by free nibbles such as *grissini* breadsticks and salami slices. The tradition of having a pre-dinner drink with light snacks quickly became part of Turin's social life and spread to other big cities in Italy.

Here an *aperitivo* doesn't mean just an aperitif (spritz, vermouth, wine etc.) but it also includes light snacks that go beyond nuts and crisps with small pizza slices, mini-pastries, cheese slices, cured meats, olives brought to your table. Prices vary from 5 to 12 euros.

In recent years, Turin (and some other cities in Northern Italy) has taken the *aperitivo* tradition a step further. Many cafes and bars offer *apericena* (aperitivo + dinner). It is served between 6pm and 9pm and includes a drink and an all-you-can-eat buffet of hot and cold appetisers. When you pay a fixed price, anything between 7 and 15 euros, you are handed your drink and a plate to fill up with whatever food you like. The plate is normally minuscule and you will have to do multiple visits to the buffet if you want to try various foods. The quality of food on offer varies from bar to bar and is rarely on par with what you get in a good restaurant but an *apericena* is more about the atmosphere. It is popular with students, young professionals and locals that want to have a light casual meal while socialising without breaking the bank. Many bars and cafes do not serve only drinks during the *apericena* hours, so you will have to pay the full fixed price whether you eat or not. Arrive at the bar early if you want to find a full buffet rather than leftovers.

La Farmacia Del Cambio

Address: Piazza Carignano, 2, 10123 Turin.
Tel.: 0039 011 546690.
Opening hours: Every day, 9am – 9.30pm.
www.delcambio.it/farmacia

Part of the one-Michelin-star restaurant Del Cambio, this 19th century pharmacy has been turned into a sophisticated bar-café for gourmands. Uniformed staff open the door and usher you to a table in a spacious room with opulent décor and the open restaurant kitchen. Excellent cocktails (try Vermouth antico with Mojito ice cubes or Saint Germain al Margarita with salt and pepper!) are accompanied by gourmet mini-snacks such as ceviche, meatballs, toasted almonds, deep-fried crackers of various flavours, ginger-spiked crunchy beans. Prices range from 12 to 20 euros (and higher if you order a glass of good champagne). In summer, you can sit at a table outside and admire the stunning Piazza Carignano.

Caffè San Carlo

Address: Piazza S. Carlo, 156, 10123 Turin
Opening hours: Every day, 8am – 9pm.

One of the grand historic cafes in the city, the 19th century San Carlo runs an *apericena* from 6pm to 8.30pm. A rich buffet is served in the splendid rooms decorated with red velvet chairs, imposing pillars, crystal Murano chandeliers, marble floors and gilded mirrors. For 12 euros you can get a drink and plentiful canapes, salads, pasta dishes, cured meats and cheeses.

Floris House Café

Address: Via Cavour, 16, 10123 Turin.
Tel.: 0039 011 812 6909. www.floris-profumi.it
Opening hours: Tuesday – Saturday 10.30am – 9.30pm,
Sunday 10.30 – 8pm. Closed on Monday.

Stepping inside this 18th-century palace, you might think you got the address wrong. It is a shop filled with perfumes, candles, objets d'art, furniture and fashion accessories but follow through a side door and you will find a tiny cosy café that locals love. Between 6pm and 8pm you can enjoy a gin and tonic, margarita, mojito or a glass of good wine and feast on small portions of smoked salmon, polenta slices smothered in a blue-cheese sauce, couscous and pâté. An *aperitivo* here costs 16-25 euros.

Cantina Arancia di Mezzanotte

Address: Piazza Emanuele Filiberto, 11, 10122 Turin.
Tel.: 0039 011 5211338. www.aranciadimezzanotte.it
Opening hours: Tuesday – Sunday 7pm – 1am. Closed on Monday.

Located in the lively neighbourhood of *Quadrilatero Romano*, this wine bar serves an excellent apericena for 12 euros with many traditional regional dishes. Choose from their 200 wines or numerous cocktails that come with a dozen of snacks served at the table and include a warm *bagna cauda* dip with raw vegetables, *vitello tonnato*, salami, pickles, cheeses, the old-fashioned hard-boiled eggs and pasta.

02 VEAL WITH A FISH SAUCE, PICKLED COURGETTES AND STUFFED PEACHES

My name is Rosemarie Scavo and I have been living in Turin for almost eight years now. I moved here from Australia to teach English for what I thought would be a year. For various reasons (amongst others, falling in love with a local and the city!) I ended up staying. These days, whenever I have a spare moment from the day job and running after a toddler, I blog about food and cooking at www.turinmamma.com

Favourite dishes: Piedmont is famous for its variety of *antipasti*. It is not uncommon for a host to serve five at a meal here! My favourites are *vitello tonnato* and *zucchine in carpione*. I am also very fond of Piedmontese desserts such as *pesche ripiene* (stuffed peaches). And, of course *grissini* and *gianduiotti* chocolates!

Vitello tonnato – see page 10.

Zucchine in carpione – slices of zucchini fried and marinated in vinegar with garlic and onion. Traditionally served as an appetiser or side dish with meat.

Pesche ripiene – baked peaches stuffed with a filling of amaretti biscuits, butter, eggs and chocolate. Served warm or cold.

Grissini - locals will tell you that *grissini* breadsticks were invented in Turin in the 17th century. The city's bakeries are home to an incredible variety of breadsticks. Locals snack on them during the day or before a meal and use them crushed for stuffing or to coat meat.

Gianduiotti – chocolates made with cocoa and hazelnuts are legendary. This chocolate-hazelnut mix distinct to Turin and Piedmont appears to have been born due to a naval blockade of the Mediterranean. The cost of importing cocoa into French-occupied Piedmont had become astronomically high. In 1852, Michele Prochet, a local chocolate maker came up with the idea of extending the small amount of chocolate he had by mixing it with hazelnuts from the Langhe area. It was a mix born out of the economic necessities of the time, but it turned out to be a winning combination.

Why: I like *vitello tonnato* for its distinct meat-fish combination; *zucchini in carpione* for the sweet-sour flavour and the fact that it can be served cold (often with a piece of fish or meat in it); stuffed peaches because of the simplicity of preparing these and the flavours involved. I think gorging on *gianduiotti* and enjoying grissini breadsticks are truly essential food experiences in Turin.

Where: I like several restaurants which serve traditional Piedmontese food in Turin but the truth is, these days, I prefer 'staying in' and cooking these dishes myself or enjoying them at my friends' homes. Right now, eating out is not the most relaxing experience with my little daughter Camilla in tow!

L'ACINO € €

Address: Via San Domenico 2/A, 10122 Turin
Tel: 0039 0115217077
Opening hours: Tuesday – Sunday, 7.30pm – 11pm.
Closed on Monday.

The restaurant's short menu features excellent seasonal dishes from different corners of Piedmont such as the snails from Cherasco with cherry tomatoes (*lumache di Cherasco con pomodorini*), rabbit cooked in a local white wine Arneis (*coniglio all'Arneis*), *vitello tonnato alla moda antica* and *zucchine in carpione*. The place is small and popular with locals and tourists alike, so make sure to make a reservation.

Le Antiche Sere € €

Address: Via Cenischia, 9, 10139 Turin

Tel: 0039 011 3854347

Opening hours: Monday – Saturday, 8pm – 10.30pm.

Closed on Sunday.

For more see page 12.

Sotto La Mole € €

Address: Via Montebello, 9, 10124 Turin

Tel. 0039 011 8179398;

Opening hours: Tuesday – Sunday 12.30-2pm, 7.30-10pm.

Closed on Monday. www.sottolamole.eu

Pricey but in a strategic location – under the Mole Antonelliana – and a great option for special occasions! The tasting menu features delicious *agnolotti* pasta, slowly cooked pork cheeks and an exquisite selection of artisan cheeses served with a traditional *cognà* mixed fruit marmalade. Rosemarie suggests trying their excellent *tapulone* (donkey stew, a specialty of northeastern Piedmontese town of Borgamanero).

Perino Vesco bakery

Address: Via Camillo Benso di Cavour, 10, 10123 Turin

Opening hours: Monday – Saturday 7.30am – 7.30pm.

Closed on Sunday.

Rosemarie says that this bakery makes absolutely amazing *grissini*. For more see "Bakeries that locals love" on page 90.

Farina Nel Sacco bakery

Address: Via Andrea Massena, 11/C, 10128 Turin

Opening hours: Monday – Saturday 7.30am – 7.30pm.

Closed on Sunday.

Apart from excellent breads, you can also buy a wide range of crunchy delicious savoury and sweet *grissini* (I loved the ones with cacao!). For more see "Bakeries that locals love" on page 90.

A. GIORDANO

Address: P.zza Carlo Felice, 69, 10123 Turin
Opening hours: Monday 3 – 7.30pm, Tuesday – Saturday 8am – 8pm
Closed on Sunday. www.giordanocioccolato.it

Family-run and filled to the brim with chocolates and other sweet delights (for more see "Addresses for chocolate lovers" on page 24).

GUIDO GOBINO

Address: Via Lagrange, 1, 10123 Turin
Opening hours: Monday 3pm – 8pm, Tuesday – Sunday 10am – 8pm.
www.guidogobino.it

Chocolatier Guido Gobino is often called "the *gianduiotto* king" for his delicious *gianduiotto* chocolates made only with Piedmont hazelnuts (for more see "Addresses for chocolate lovers" on page 24).

Favourite places for breakfast: You should order a *brioche* (the generic term they use for croissants and other pastries here in Turin) with a *cappuccino* or *latte macchiato* and consume them standing up at the bar. At **Caffè Corner** they make excellent pastries and I often stop by here on my way to work.

CAFFÈ CORNER

Address: Corso Vittorio Emanuele II, 100, 10121 Turin
Opening hours: Every day, 6am – 10pm.

This centrally located buzzy café is popular with locals who stop here for breakfast, a slice of pizza at lunch or a glass of wine after work.

Favourite ice cream shops: I know **Grom** is Turin's most famous gelataria but I think it is also worth mentioning other ice cream shops here that have not become franchises.

GELATERIA MENODICIOTTO

Address: Piazza Castello, 54, 10122 Turin

Opening hours: Monday 12pm – 12am,

Tuesday – Thursday 9am – 12am, Friday – Saturday 9am – 1am,

Sunday 9am – 12am. www.meno18.com

This ice cream parlour with Slow Food movement's philosophy uses milk from their own farm, free-range eggs and fresh seasonal fruit. There are always several flavours for vegetarians and vegans. Try their luscious *affogato* (a scoop of ice cream topped with espresso), amazing chocolate sorbet or, for an extra filling treat, a croissant filled with generous scoops of ice cream.

GELATERIA MIRETTI

Address: Corso Giacomo Matteotti, 5, 10121 Turin

Opening hours: Monday - Saturday 7am – 1am, Sunday 8am – 2pm. www.gelateriamiretti.it

Locals are happy to queue to get ice cream here for a reason; the flavours, be they classic, exotic or seasonal, are exquisite. The shop is famous for its old-style *affogato all'amarena* which was popular in the city in the 1960s (a scoop of plain milk ice cream is drowned in cherry syrup). For the adventurous palates, there are other interesting *affogati* such as Monaco (raspberry and lemon ice cream topped with beer) and Bellini-G (peach ice cream swimming in prosecco, yummmm!).

Rosemarie's favourite gelato here is *nocciolino di Chivasso* with tiny amaretti-like biscuits made with hazelnuts, which are a specialty of the town of Chivasso, located 15km northeast of Turin.

Gelateria Alberto Marchetti

Address: Corso Vittorio Emanuele II, 24bis, 10123 Turin

Opening hours: Monday – Thursday 12pm – 12am,

Friday-Saturday 12pm – 1am, Sunday 11 am – 11pm.

www.albertomarchetti.it

If you are feeling like trying something new, Rosemarie recommends tasting the *farina bona* (which is an ice cream made with toasted polenta meal!).

Tip from a local: If you are in Turin in summer, try a gianduia-flavoured ice cream instead of chocolates. It is made with artisanal chocolate hazelnut spread that inspired Nutella.

Grissini breadsticks

ADDRESSES FOR CHOCOLATE LOVERS

Often called the European capital of chocolate, Turin is a chocolate lover's heaven. No other Italian city boasts such a high number of chocolatiers' and cafes serving decadent rich chocolate drinks. The royal house of Savoy started Turin's love affair with the sweet delight when, according to historians, the Duke of Savoy Emanuele Filiberto brought some cocoa beans home from Spain in the 16th century. By the 17th century, bourgeois families were enjoying hot chocolate served in elegant cafes all over the city. The 18th century brought technological advances that allowed production of solid chocolate and local workshops were churning out over 300 kilos a day. France, Austria, Belgium, Switzerland and Germany loved Turin's chocolate and sent their chocolatiers to the city to learn the secrets of the trade. Many artisan chocolate makers still use centuries-old recipes that are kept secret. Here is a list, far from exhaustive, based on the suggestions from the locals I interviewed and my personal research that sent my blood sugar levels skyrocketing.

Guido Gobino

Address: Via Lagrange 1, 10123 Turin
Tel. 0039 011 56 60707
Opening hours: Monday 3pm – 8pm, Tuesday – Sunday 10am – 8pm.
Address: Via Cagliari, 15/b, 10153 Turin tel. +39 011 24 762 45
Opening hours: Monday – Friday 8.30am – 12.30, 2.30pm – 6pm,
Saturday 8.30am – 12.30pm. Closed on Sunday.
www.guidogobino.it

The new generation chocolatier, Guido Gobino is famous for his meticulously researched ingredients, love of high quality single-origin chocolate and sleek modern packaging. He is often called "the *gianduiotto* king" for skilfully combining the traditional recipe with innovative techniques that results in an exceptionally delicious and wide range of *gianduiotto* chocolates made only with Piedmont hazelnuts. His other signature product, Cialdine Bitter Extra Blend, travelled to space in 2013 as treats for the astronauts on the mission. If you are after unusual flavours try Gobino's tiny ganache chocolates with Barolo, vermouth, lemon and cloves or eucalyptus (flavours change with seasons) or *cremino al sale* with hazelnut paste, sea salt and olive oil. You can book a guided visit of the Gobino factory on Via Cagliari (mornings only, 8 euros per person, minimum 10 people) or a chocolate degustation in the café at the back of the shop in Via Lagrange (15-25 euros per person).

Guido Castagna

Address: Via Maria Vittoria, 27/C, 10123 Turin
Opening hours: Monday 3.30 – 7.30,
Tuesday – Saturday 10.30am – 1.30pm, 3.00 – 7.30pm,
Sunday 9.30am – 1.30pm.
www.guidocastagna.it
Step inside this small sleek chocolate boutique to discover delightful creations of another local young chocolatier who is committed to sourcing only ethically harvested cocoa beans. Maestro Castagna uses his own slow delicate method to make excellent chocolates that have won him many international awards. He believes that chocolate, like wine, requires time and matures it for at least 6 months before turning it into exquisite products. Connoisseurs will appreciate Castagna's raw chocolate Madagascar and Venezuela bars.

A. Giordano

Address: Piazza Carlo Felice, 69, 10123 Turin
Opening hours: Monday 3 – 7.30pm, Tuesday – Saturday 8am – 8pm
Closed on Sunday.
www.giordanocioccolato.it
Entering this family-run shop is like stepping back in time. Filled to the brim with sweet delights, A. Giordano is famous for its award-winning *Giacometti*, a delectable mix of chocolate and hazelnuts shaped strictly by hand into little rough pyramids. Their original creations include *Alpinluce* chocolates filled with the sweet wine *Erbaluce di Caluso* and *preferiti ricoperti*, local cherries soaked in *maraschino* liquor and hand-rolled in chocolate. The classic *cremini Torino* in retro-style wrappings will make a lovely gift for anyone with a sweet tooth.

Stratta

Address: Piazza San Carlo, 191, 10123 Turin.
Opening hours: Tuesday – Saturday 9am – 7pm,
Sunday 9.30am – 7pm. Closed on Monday.
www.stratta1836.it

Locals call this pretty confectioner's shop "the sitting room of Turin" because of its central location. Making sweet delights since 1836, the shop still has a charming retro feel with its gilded décor, chandeliers and bright vintage-style packaging. The Savoy house crest is proudly displayed on the shop's main wall to commemorate the fact that Stratta was once the official supplier of the Royal Family. Their *gianduiotti* are among the best in the city (they also have a sugar-free version). I liked their *tronchetti alle noci* with chestnut and rum filling as well as *alchechengi al cioccolato* (chocolate-covered winter cherry). They also make the most delightful colourful bon-bons and meringues with chocolate.

Platti

Address: Corso Vittorio Emanuele II, 72, 10121 Turin
Opening hours: Every day 7.30am – 9pm
www.platti.it

If you are a hot chocolate connoisseur, head to this elegant historic café, which serves the most decadent rich drinks flavoured with liquors or topped with whipped cream. I loved their hot chocolate with Cointreau and orange peel that arrived accompanied by a small plate of exquisite bite-sized biscuits and a glass of fizzy water (in case of a sugar overdose or just to clear the palate before digging into a slice of cake). Not cheap at 6-7 euros a cup, but it is certainly worth it.

Peyrano

Address: Corso Moncalieri, 47, 10133 Turin
Opening hours: Monday – Friday 9 – 12.30pm, 1.30 – 6pm
Address: Corso Vittorio Emanuele II, 76, 101201 Turin Opening
hours: Tuesday – Saturday 9am – 7pm
www.ilgiustodelcioccolato.it

A household name in Turin and Italy, Peyrano has been making chocolate since 1915. One of their signature products is the classic *alpino* with a hazelnut cream and *grappa* filling made to a secret recipe. Their *gianduiotto antica formula*, hugely popular with locals, has a high percentage of hazelnuts and a unique subtle smoky flavour that comes from the olive tree wood used to roast the cocoa beans. Another locals' favourite is the torta Peyrano, a cake filled with chocolate cream, orange marmalade and coated with dark chocolate. For a Willy Wonka experience, book a guided tour of the Peyrano chocolate factory on Corso Moncalieri via their website. In summer, you can enjoy Peyrano organic chocolate ice cream in their café on Corso Vittorio Emanuele II.

Gianduiotti chocolates

03 DESIGNER COCKTAILS, ICE CREAM AND SOCIAL EATING

My name is Anna Scudellari. I moved to Turin from the Emilia Romagna region 19 years ago. I work as a consultant in the Corporate Heritage sector and run social eating events at home. I love having people in my house and exchanging experiences and stories at the table. (You can find Anna's page on Gnammo website: https://gnammo.com/annouka).

Favourite dishes: *carne cruda battuta al coltello*, risotto, ice cream and chocolate.

> ***Carne cruda battuta al coltello*** – a local version of steak tartare, raw veal, normally of the prized Fassone breed, typical for Piedmont, finely chopped with a knife. It is seasoned with olive oil, lemon juice, salt and pepper. Served as an appetiser.

Why: I did not know about the *carne cruda* before moving to Turin as in my native region there is nothing like it, so it was a real discovery for me! Ice cream is a classic in the city: there are many brands, with each of them trying to differentiate themselves with better quality and ingredients, so there is ice cream for any taste and palate here. With regards to chocolate, it is impossible to ignore it in Turin! From *bicerin* (a hot drink made with espresso, drinking chocolate, milk and served in a small glass – for more see page 35) to the famous *gianduiotti* chocolates – this huge gluttonous variety has conquered me from the moment I moved to the city. I love the tiny *gianduiotti* Tourinot that melt in your mouth from **Guido Gobino** (for more see "Addresses for chocolate lovers" on page 24)

(for more see "Addresses for chocolate lovers" on page 24)

Tip from a local: Locals eat chocolate only during cold months of the year, not in summer!

Where:

BOTTEGA BARETTI €€

Address: Via Sant'Anselmo, 28, 10125 Turin

Tel. 0039 011 7900331

Opening hours: Sunday – Thursday 7.30pm – 12.30am,

Friday – Saturday 7.30pm – 1am.

www.bottegabaretti.com

A lively restaurant that takes pride in high quality ingredients sourced from small local producers. Apart from excellent pizza you can devour chicken and beef burgers, salads and bruschetta. Meat lovers will enjoy *La Grissinopoli*, a juicy cut of *Fassone* veal coated with crushed *grissini* breadsticks. Anna says their *carne cruda* (on the menu it is listed as *Tartare di Fassone*) is especially good and is served with creamy spiced *stracciatella* cheese and toasted bread chips. On the menu you will see recommendations for pairing the dishes with beer.

Favourite places for breakfast: Anna likes the small **Orso Laboratorio Caffè** that has an excellent choice of premium quality coffee blends from different countries.

Orso Laboratorio Caffè

Address: Via Claudio Luigi Berthollet, 30h, 10125 Turin.

Opening hours: Tuesday – Sunday, 6.30am – 6pm.

Closed on Monday.

A paradise for coffee connoisseurs! Here it is all about the quality, mix and roast of the coffee beans. The pastries are fresh from the bakery nearby and milk comes from a local producer. On the bottom of your coffee cup you will find a number that you can look up on a list at the bar that will give you mystic predictions and pearls of wisdom. There are many coffee varieties here, do not be afraid to ask the friendly staff for advice. For lunch choose from a wide range of fresh panini sandwiches. Prices from 1,10 to 4 euros for a cup of coffee.

Favourite ice cream shops: Anna loves the *fior di latte* ice cream from **Agrigelateria San Pé** for its clean authentic flavour.

Agrigelateria San Pé

Address: EATALY, Via Nizza 230, 10126 Turin.

Opening hours: Every day, 10am – 10.30pm.

www.agrigelateria.eu

Ice cream is made using traditional methods from milk and fruit that come from the owners' farm located a short drive from Turin. In the city, you can find them in EATALY or make it a day trip and drive to the farm in Poirino.

Other suggestions: Locals love *apericena*, aperitif + dinner, offered in bars from 6pm to 8pm (see "Turin-style aperitivo and apericena" on page 10). There are many options in Turin. I like the **Smile Tree** bar with their dramatically presented cocktails and vegan menu.

SMILE TREE BAR

Address: Piazza della Consolata 9/c, 10122 Turin

Opening hours: Tuesday – Saturday 7pm – 2am,

Sunday 7pm – 12am. Closed on Monday.

www.smiletree.it

Each cocktail is like a movie set! Unusual flavours, tiny clouds of smoke and fog, slabs of marble, smoked fruit – the famous cocktail designer Dennis Zoppi, the bar owner, knows how to impress. With more than 200 cocktails on the menu you will be spoilt for choice. Apart from the printed menu, you can also ask to see the list on their iPad, which has photos and explanations.

Cocktail at Smile Tree

DINE AT THE HOME OF A LOCAL

Want to eat with locals at their homes? It is easier than you think! Social eating is a new trend bringing people together at a dinner table with local chefs opening their homes for food lovers. Often described as "Airbnbs for eating", Gnammo, BonAppetour, Le Cesarine, have been successful and reliable online platforms for meal sharing experiences for several years. You can search the websites by your destination and see what dinners are scheduled for the dates that suit you, read the chef's profile, reviews by previous guests and see the menu. The dinner menus often feature traditional local or regional Italian dishes as well as ethnic food. Most of the home chefs are amateurs with a passion for cooking who want to meet new people and share their love for food. They do not make much money with their dinner parties, just enough to pay for the ingredients and a little extra. Places can be booked directly on the websites. Prices range from 15 to 50 euros.

Gnammo

www.gnammo.com

The Italian-based website, offers many options for social eating in Turin. If you cannot find anything for the required date, check out the option "Menu on demand" that allows you to contact the chef and see if it is possible to organise a particular dinner party for you. In the listings, you can see the minimum number of guests required for a booking.

BonAppetour

www.bonappetour.com

The site lists dinner party hosts in more than 80 cities on six continents who offer in-home food experiences for travellers. There are several home chefs based in Turin and small towns nearby.

Le Cesarine

www.cesarine.it

A small social eating platform with a strong focus on Italian regional cuisine. Guests can participate in dinner preparation in cooks' homes. As I was writing this book, only two hosts were available in Turin, both offering excellent traditional menus.

Cooking with locals in Turin

Want to learn how to make traditional dishes from Piedmont?

Our cooking classes take place at local families' homes.
Your hosts will teach you how to make typical
antipasti, primi, secondi and dolci.

After the class, you will have a big lunch eating
what you cooked with other tasty additions.

For more details go to
WWW.ITALYWITHGUSTO/COOKING
or email CLASSES@ITALYWITHGUSTO.COM

04 GOOD WINE, SLOW FAST FOOD AND THE BICERIN DRINK... WITHOUT THE CROWD

My name is Diana Zahuranec, and I've been living in Italy for almost five years, in Turin for three. I came to Italy from the United States to attend the University of Gastronomic Sciences in Pollenzo for a Master's degree in Food Culture and Communications. Now I work as the English editor, journalist, and translator with an online wine tourism magazine in Piedmont called Wine Pass (www.winepassitaly.it), which is based in Alba in the Langhe.

Favourite dishes: *Tajarin*, a long pasta made with as many as a dozen egg yolks or more, in a simple sauce of butter, sage, and Parmigiano; or (more of an Alba specialty), with white truffle shaved over top or made into a creamy sauce. *Carne cruda*, beef tartare, or...raw meat! It took me several years to actually like this, but my taste buds finally understood that it is amazing. It is seasoned with salt and pepper and drizzled with extra virgin olive oil, with a few shavings of Parmigiano or truffle on top if you're lucky. *Bicerin*, a chocolate drink invented in Turin. *Bagna cauda*, a warm dip made from anchovies, garlic, and extra virgin olive oil, served with roasted peppers or fresh veggies. It is just as potent and savoury as it sounds. And if you're feeling more daring, the *finanziera*, a very flavourful rich dish. And food, of course, is only made better with wine! I always want friends and family to try a nebbiolo. A Barolo or a Barbaresco are top choices, but if you don't want to spend so much on a bottle, just get a glass at a good wine bar; or order a Nebbiolo d'Alba, Roero DOCG, or other nebbiolo wine. I love the nebbiolo wines from northern Piedmont, like Gattinara, Ghemme, or Boca.

Tajarin ai 40 tuorli – thin flat pasta made with 40 egg yolks per kilo of flour. The best tajarin pasta is made strictly by hand, without the use of a rolling machine and no added liquid, only flour, yolks and a pinch of salt. Classic sauces include butter and white truffle shavings, pork and veal or porcini mushroom sauce.

Carne cruda – see page 28.

Bicerin – one of the city's gastronomic symbols, this layered hot drink made of chocolate, espresso, cream is served in a glass. Some locals will tell you that *bicerin* was the drink of the Italian unification as Count Camillo Benso di Cavour, the central figure of the *Risorgimento*, and his associates drank endless glasses of it while debating the future of the country. Today, many cafes serve the drink topped with whipped cream, which makes old Turin residents and gastronomic traditionalists cringe because the original recipe calls for liquid thick cream. Another sign of a good *bicerin* is clearly visible layers of the ingredients. The drink doesn't come cheap, expect to pay 5-6 euros for a glass.

Bagna cauda– see page 11.

Finanziera – an ancient dish dating back to medieval times from the Monferrato area that is becoming more and more difficult to find in Turin's restaurants. This stew is made with cocks' crests, chicken liver, calf brain and sweetbreads, all slowly cooked with Marsala or red wine, a small amount of vinegar and thickened with a pinch of flour. The recipe was invented out of a need to use up the bits that had no commercial value and could not be sold at the city markets. In the 19th century the tasty dish of the poor became fashionable and was served in the exclusive **Cambio restaurant** (Piazza Carignano, 2, 10123 Turin) to important state employees and Prime Minister Cavour who were all very fond of it.

Where: As they're Piedmontese specialties, you'll be able to find them anywhere around Turin (although for the *tajarin* with white truffle, you're better off in Alba; I also had a great plate of it in Bra at a restaurant called Il **Bagnet** (Via Cherasco, 1, Bra).

The café that invented the bicerin is called **Al Bicerin**, and it is very good there, but it is always crowded. I prefer the bicerin served at **Caffè Fiorio**. It is a beautiful, elegant place on two floors with red velvet chairs, where diplomats and nobles once sat to discuss politics. They serve it with whipped cream, which is apparently not traditional, but I will happily take whipped cream over frothed milk.

I am still exploring the world of *carne cruda*, but I believe it would be very good at **Fassoneria**, a restaurant that specializes in burgers in the Quadrilatero district (the Ancient Roman quarters of the city). Another good restaurant with great ambiance is the **Porto di Savona**, which serves many different traditional Piedmontese dishes, and where you can pre-order the *bagna cauda*. I've tried the *finanziera* at **Ristorante Consorzio** and thought it was very good, flavourful and well prepared. Before trying it I was a little hesitant about its texture, but there was nothing for me to be afraid of. I would get it again.

CAFFÈ AL BICERIN

Address: Piazza della Consolata, 5, 10122 Torino

Opening hours: 8.30am – 7.30pm, closed on Wednesday.

www.bicerin.it

Entering this small historic café is like stepping back in time: marble tables, dark wood shelves, glass jars filled with bright sweets. Many locals believe that the *bicerin* drink was invented here as the coffeehouse has been serving it since the 18th century. For a pure Turin-only experience, order a slice of bicerin cake (*la torta bicerin*) with your *bicerin* drink.

Tip from a Local: Do not mix the layers of your bicerin or the cold cream will cool down the drink.

CAFFÈ FIORIO

Address: Via Po, 8, 10121 Turin.

Opening hours: Every day 8am – 1am.

Opened in 1780, this historic café has seen many illustrious figures as customers. Apart from the hot *bicerin* drink, *zabaione* and fresh pastries, you can also have light lunch, *aperitivo* and excellent ice cream made on the premises that, according to some sources, German philosopher Friedrich Nietzsche loved. Locals credit Caffè Fiorio with the invention of the ice cream cone and breaking the taboo on women eating it in public.

Burger from Fassoneria Torino

Fassoneria €

Address: Via San Massimo, 17, 10123 Turin

Piazza Emanuele Filiberto, 4, 10122 Turin

Tel. 0039 393 858 4005; 0039 011 885543.

Opening hours: Tuesday – Sunday 12.30-2.30pm, 7.30-11.00pm. Closed on Monday.

www.fassoneriatorino.it

With farm-to-table philosophy in mind, this gourmet burger joint uses only the prized Fassone beef renowned for its low fat content and produced by a cooperative of farmers in the province of Cuneo. For more see "Addresses for meat lovers" on page 48.

Porto di Savona € €

Address: Piazza Vittorio Veneto, 2, 10123 Turin.

Tel. 0039 011817 3500

Opening hours: Every day, 12.30pm – 2.30pm, 7.30pm – 11.30pm.

The restaurant has been serving typical local dishes since 1863 when horse carriages parted for the port of Savona from its front door. The 19th century tavern-style décor is combined with traditional hearty dishes of Piedmonte. Check out the menu of the day for seasonal dishes. *Bagna cauda* is served in autumn and winter. Go for their degustation menu (*Menù degustazione*) if you want to try a range of typical regional dishes in one sitting.

Ristorante Consorzio € €

Address: Via Monte di Pietà, 23, 10122 Turin
Tel. 0039 011 2767661
Opening hours: Monday – Friday, 12.30pm-2.30pm, 7.30pm-11.00pm, Saturday 7.30pm-11.00pm. Closed on Sunday.
www.ristoranteconsorzio.it

This small busy restaurant is renowned for its good quality traditional regional dishes and Slow Food philosophy. The menu changes often but there are always the classics such as *ravioli di finanziera* (pasta filled with the *finanziera* mix), *brasato di Fassona* and *carne cruda battuta al coltello*. The extensive wine list offers a great choice of local and international labels with a focus on organic and natural wines. Booking is recommended.

Damarco wine shop

Address: Piazza della Repubblica, 4, 10122 Turin.
Tel. 0039 011 436 1086
Opening hours: Monday – Friday 8.30 – 1pm, 3.30 – 7.30pm, Saturday 8.30 – 7.30pm. Closed on Sunday and Wednesday afternoon.
www.damarcotorino.it

The family-run shop opened in 1959 and since has become the biggest enoteca in the city. Sells over 4000 wines, spirits, liqueurs from Piedmont and beyond, as well as some food specialties.

Tip from a Local: Turin is still quite non-touristy. In fact, you might not even want to go by the old rule of "avoid English menus" here. In Turin, an English menu does not necessarily mean "super-touristy / avoid," but simply that the owners had the foresight to translate for the occasional non-Italian that stops by.

Cantina Torino wine bar

Address: via Monte di Pietà 15/B, 10122 Turin

Tel. 0039 011 1971 5833

Opening hours: Tuesday – Saturday 12.30 – 11pm.

Closed on Sunday and Monday.

Diana's favourite wine bar in Turin. It has an outstanding selection of only small producers from Piedmont, friendly and knowledgeable owners, and lots of wine by the glass. You can also have lunch (from 12.30 to 3.30pm), *aperitivo* and dinner here. Excellent charcuterie and cheeses from regional farms served as *tagliere* (cheese and charcuterie boards).

Favourite ice cream shops: Turin is full of artisan gelaterie of high quality and innovative flavours. Some of my favourites that never disappoint are **Vanilla** and **Rivareno** and I could go on... At **Vanilla** I especially love their *cuneesi al Rhum* ice cream, which is chocolate and rum flavoured (named after the famous chocolates made in Cuneo), with big chunks of dark chocolate throughout. At **Rivareno** they have a *gianduja* (chocolate-hazelnut) flavour with sea salt called *GranTorino* and it is delicious.

VANILLA

Address: Via Palazzo di Città, 7B, 10122 Turin
Opening hours: Every day 12.30 – 10.30pm.

The owners of this small ice cream shop, Bruno and Simone, pride themselves on using only high quality fresh ingredients. Apart from the classics such as *fiordipanna*, there are always new seasonal and exotic delicious flavours.

New food trends in the city: There has been a movement towards "slow fast food," and I love it (Piedmont is, by the way, home of the Slow Food organization). It shows Italians' innovation as well as awareness of a work culture that does not really allow for a heavy, long lunch (the "traditional" Italian lunch used to be bigger than dinner—but this is no longer done so much). Slow fast food restaurants tend to serve a wide selection of a few kinds of food, such as panini, pasta or burgers, and proudly use Piedmontese ingredients and inspiration. I like **M**Bun, Master Sandwich** and **Fuzion** ("Italian sushi and Japanese pizza"—try it to believe how good it is).

M**BUN €

Address: Corso Giuseppe Siccardi, 8/A; Via Rattazzi 4, 10122 Turin.
Opening hours: Monday – Thursday 12pm – 11pm, Friday – Sunday 12pm – 12am. www.mbun.it

The Piedmontese answer to McDonald's, these burger joints are run by a family of meat farmers. Every single ingredient that goes into a burger here can be traced back to a local producer: Piedmontese beef, high quality pork, free-range chicken, artisan bread, vegetables from a farm not far from the city. There are several vegetarian and vegan options (e.g. a chickpea and millet burger). You will not find Coca Cola here, instead get

MoleCola, a fizzy drink made locally. Even the disposable cutlery is made from biodegradable plastic! Fast food has never been slower and better than this!

Master Sandwich €

Address: Via Palazzo di Città, 6, 10122 Turin

Opening hours: Monday – Thursday 11am – 9pm,

Friday – Saturday 11am – 11.30pm, Sunday 11am – 6.30pm

A tiny shop with a menu (also in English) that boasts over 40 types of sandwiches made with fresh regional ingredients. There are only a few seats inside and you might have to queue for a few minutes before getting served but it is worth the wait.

Fuzion €

Address: Via Dell'Accademia Albertina 29/A, 10123 Turin

Opening hours: Tuesday – Sunday 12pm – 3pm, 7pm – 11pm. Closed on Monday. www.fuzionfood.it

In this tiny restaurant chef Domenico Volgare successfully manages to combine Asian and Mediterranean cuisine. Apart from traditional noodles and slow leavened pizzas with high-quality Italian and local ingredients, you will also find such delicious original creations as pizza with shiitake mushrooms and wasabi mayo, tom yum pizza, seaweed fritters and mouth-watering meat and seafood sushi. Many options for vegetarians and vegans.

ADDRESSES FOR VEGETARIANS AND VEGANS

Although Piedmont's cuisine is rich with meat-based dishes, Turin's numerous vegetarian and vegan eateries (more than 30 at last count before this book was published) will keep all non-carnivores happy. A recently elected young mayor of the city has taken the trend even further by introducing a city council's programme to reduce the amount of animal products eaten in the region's capital and focussing on promoting vegan and vegetarian diets (naturally, the move has drawn a lot of criticism, locally and nationally).

Most non-specialised restaurants would offer several vegetarian options, however, finding vegan-friendly dishes on a regular menu might be more of a challenge. I was especially delighted to see meat- and egg-free creative interpretations of such traditional dishes as *agnolotti del plin* or Russian salad in some specialised restaurants. Many ice cream shops sell delicious vegetarian and vegan gelato while in most city centre bars you can ask for a cappuccino with soya milk and vegan croissants.

Mezzaluna €

Address: Piazza Emanuele Filiberto 8/D, 10122 Turin
Tel. 0039 011 4367622
Opening hours: Monday – Wednesday 9am – 7.30 pm, Thursday – Saturday 9am – 11pm. Closed on Sunday.
www.mezzalunabio.it

Open since 1994, long before the vegetarian-vegan trend arrived to the city, Mezzaluna is a restaurant, cafe, and organic food shop. On the menu, you will find meat-free ravioli del plin, an egg-free version of Russian salad, hemp pasta with vegetables and many other dishes that vary depending on the season. There is also a great range of excellent cakes, many of them raw and sugar-free. You can get a take-out in the deli.

Soul Kitchen – Vegan & Raw Restaurant €

Address: Via Santa Giulia, 2, 10124 Turin
Tel. 0039 011 884700
Opening hours: Tuesday – Saturday 12.30 – 2.30pm, 7.30 – 10.30pm. Closed on Sunday and Monday. www.thesoulkitchen.it

Often mentioned as one of the best of its kind in Italy, this trendy restaurant adds a gourmet twist to vegan cuisine. The menu changes monthly and never features anything with sugar or refined commercial flours. The portions can be small but are always full of flavour. One of their most popular desserts is the delectable raw chocolate cake. The restaurant gets busy in the evening, so it would be wise to make a reservation before heading there.

Exki €

Address: via dell'Arcivescovado 2/E, 10121 Turin
Opening hours: Monday – Friday 7.30am – 7.30pm,
Saturday 9am – 7.30pm, Sunday 9.30am – 7.30pm.
Address: Via Pietro Micca 2/H, 10122 Turin
Opening hours: Monday – Friday 7.30am – 6.30pm,
Saturday – Sunday 9am – 7.30pm
Other locations: via Nizza 262/62B, via Carlo Alberto 29/B, Corso Vittorio Emanuele II 98/N, via Principi d'Acaja 32.
www.exki.it

This is a chain of organic Belgian restaurant-cafés with six locations across the city (there are also Exki restaurants in Milan, many cities in France, Netherlands and the U.S.A.). Although not everything on the menu is vegetarian, you will find a good range of freshly made salads, soups, panini, quiches, smoothies and cakes. Do not expect gourmet dishes or an especially warm atmosphere. It is a great option if you are looking for a quick meal or a take-out.

Cheesecake in MiaGola Caffè

MiaGola Caffè €

Address: Via Giovanni Amendola 6D, 10121 Turin
Tel. 0039 011 0371375
Opening hours: Monday – Friday 10am – 8pm,
Saturday – Sunday 10am – 8.30pm. www.miagolacaffe.it

This is certainly one of my favourite vegetarian/vegan cafés in Turin and not only because they have six resident cats (yes, it is a cat café, the first one in Italy). I love their excellent herbal tea blends (with lovely cat-themed names such as "I lick my whiskers", "Let's play with a ball of yarn", "Desire for cuddles") and cakes. There is a large screen where you can watch videos of dogs available for adoptions in the city's shelters. On Saturday and Sunday, the café gets quite busy during their buffet style brunch. The fat resident cats are lazy, happy and rather indifferent to the people around them (to the dismay of some customers who come here more for cat cuddles than for food).

Il Gelato Amico

Address: Via San Massimo, 34, 10123 Turin
Opening hours: Tuesday - Sunday 11.30am – 10pm,
Monday 11.30am – 8pm. www.ilgelatoamico.it

Centrally located but easy to miss, this small gelateria sells only vegan ice cream made with rice milk. There are always at least ten flavours on offer, with something new added every month. Apart from the classic hazelnut, pistachio, almond, dark chocolate you will always find unusual flavours such as lemon and sage, goji berry, apple and ginger. All ice creams are gluten-free and made without any synthetic additives or refined sugar (stevia and other natural sweeteners are used instead). They also sell exquisite ice cream cakes in different sizes and their version of the locally popular chocolate *Sacher* cake is divine!

I am Paola Forneris. I live in the province of Turin but love the city and visit it frequently. I work in human resources and in my spare time run a food and travel blog called Viaggi e Delizie (www.viaggiedelizie.com).

Favourite dishes: One of the typical dishes in Turin that I like is *tonno di coniglio*, rabbit cooked slowly with herbs which makes it as soft as tuna, hence the name. One of my favourite desserts is *Pinguino gelato*, a rich ice cream on a stick covered with chocolate.

Tonno di coniglio – the name of this dish is loosely translated as tuna-style rabbit with the word "tuna" referring to the consistency of the meat and the fact that it is preserved in olive oil. Rabbit is boiled for over an hour with garlic, onions, herbs and vegetables and cooled down. The meat is then torn off the bones, seasoned with sage, garlic and salt and left immersed in extra virgin olive oil for 2-3 days. As it can be stored for up to 10 days, the dish was popular among peasants during busy harvest times.

Pinguino gelato – the Gelati Pepino company created the world's first chocolate-covered ice cream on a stick in 1939 and since then it has become somewhat of Torino's symbol and one of the most popular treats in the city. The ice cream is quite small by modern standards, only 70g, and comes in different flavours such as coffee, mint, hazelnut, coconut, gianduja (chocolate-hazelnut spread) and the classic cream.

Why: I like the rabbit dish because it is about local traditions, cooked with very few ingredients and delicious. The *Pinguino* ice cream reminds me of my childhood, when I visited my aunt and uncle in Turin and we went for walks around the city. Nowadays, every time I am in the city centre, I try to go to the Pepino ice cream shop on Piazza Carignano.

Where: *Tonno di coniglio* is good in the restaurant **Quanto Basta**.

Quanto Basta € €
Address: Via San Domenico 12-b, 10122 Turin.
Tel. 0039 011 521 4452
Opening hours: Thursday – Tuesday, 12 – 3pm, 7.30 – 11pm.
Closed on Wednesday. www.quantobastaristorante.it
A modern centrally located restaurant run by two friends. Apart from the à la carte menu there is a degustation menu with typical dishes of Torino. The menu changes every month and always features a choice of meat, fish, vegetarian and gluten-free dishes.

Baravan € €
Address: Via Principe Tommaso, 16, 10125 Turin.
Tel. 0039 342 9470459
Opening hours: Monday – Saturday, 8am – 11pm.
Closed on Sunday. www.baravanristorante.it
Bistrot-style bar-restaurant that serves an interesting mix of classic local and Asian dishes. The wine list features organic, biodynamic and small lesser-known wine producers. Seasonal menu. Paola especially likes the exotic sweet and sour flavours of the *gamberoni in gabbia* dish in this restaurant.

Bar Café Pepino
Address: Piazza Carignano, 8, 10123 Turin
Opening hours: Tuesday – Thursday 9.30am – 10.30pm, Friday –

Once a supplier for the House of Savoy, this family-run business has been making excellent gelato since 1884. In 1939, it became famous for inventing the *Pinguino*, a small chocolate covered ice cream on a stick that is still very popular with locals. The small cosy bar has the classic old style décor with wood panels, red velvet seats and small marble tables. You can sit outside to admire the spectacular Piazza Carignano on warmer days. For lunch, the bar serves good quality pasta dishes and salads. Some local supermarkets stock Pepino ice cream. Keep an eye out for their logoed white and blue fridges. Recently, Pepino has opened a new centrally located ice cream shop, **La Pinguineria** (Via Rattazzi, 3B, 10123 Turin) which sells their signature flavours.

ADDRESSES FOR MEAT LOVERS

Carnivores among you will want to stay in Turin forever! Many traditional dishes here are meat-based and servings are generous. However, it is not only the portion size that will make you jump with joy. The quality of meat in the city is second to none. Torinesi love the Fassone beef for which Piedmont is famous, so you will find it in many good restaurants and gourmet fast food joints. The prized beef is lower in fat than conventional types, more tender and is often called "the Rolls Royce of beef".

If you want to taste the best meat dishes that Turin has to offer, try *carne battuto* (see page 28), *finanziera* (see page 35), *brasato al Barolo* (see page 69), *fricandò di carne* (traditional meat and potato stew), *bollito misto* (different cuts of slow-cooked beef mixed with less noble bits such as tail and cotechino as well as pieces of boiled capon and pork served with different sauces). If you are up for a taste challenge, you may want to brave *fritto misto alla piemontese*, an ancient traditional peasant dish that is harder to find nowadays. It consists of battered deep-fried veal, lamb and pig sweetbreads, liver, brains, kidneys, lungs, all served on one plate together with fried apple slices, sweet amaretto biscuits, sweet polenta and vegetables. Certainly not for the faint-hearted!

Fassoneria €€

Address: Via San Massimo, 17, 10123 Turin
Piazza Emanuele Filiberto, 4, 10122 Turin
Tel. 0039 393 858 4005; 0039 011 885543;
Opening hours: Tuesday – Sunday 12.30-2.30pm, 7.30-11.00pm. Closed on Monday. www.fassoneriatorino.it

With farm-to-table philosophy in mind, this gourmet burger joint uses only Italian ingredients, including the prized Fassone beef produced by a cooperative of farmers in the province of Cuneo. The meat is cooked within 24 hours of arrival from the producer. The menu features over 20 types of burgers with seasonal ingredients, salads, delicious potato fries and some excellent artisan beers. Eat in or take out. Prices range from 6 to 12 euros.

MuUrgheria €€

Address: Via Nizza, 129/A, 10126 Turin
Opening hours: Monday – Friday 12.30 – 3pm, 7.30 – 10.30pm; 7.30pm – 11.30pm. Closed on Sunday

Another great example of slow fast food in Turin. The Fassone beef used to make hamburgers here comes from a farm in Villanova d'Asti that has won some impressive titles at national and international agricultural shows. On the menu you will also find chicken burgers made with the meat of a rare heirloom breed, the Bionda Piemontese. The menu features more than 20 types of burgers, many classics as well as creative gourmet options, with the Muu Dello Chef updated weekly: burgers with ricotta, fig and mustard sauce, with truffle cream and mascarpone cheese, with green beans, strawberries and a mint sauce. Their 300g triple Muusuperburger will make any hungry carnivore happy! All burgers come with potato fries. There is also a small range of organic ice creams, good wines and artisan beers. Prices range from 6 to 11 euros. Eat in or take out.

La Locanda del Sorriso €€

Address: Via Saluzzo, 6, 10125 Turin. Tel.: 0039 011 659 6142.
Opening hours: Wednesday – Monday 12 – 2.30pm, 7 – 11pm.
Closed on Tuesday. www.lalocandadelsorriso.it

The owners of this restaurant are of Calabrian origin, so the menu features many specialties from the southern region, however, every Thursday evening is devoted to the best traditional dishes of Piedmont: *bollito misto* with seven types of meat, *bagna cauda*. It is one of very few restaurants in Turin where you can still try the famous *fritto misto* without having to order the dish several days in advance, just turn up on a Thursday evening and eat to your heart's content. Here you will also find hearty *finanziera* Piemontese and a very rare ancient regional dish called *"Subric del Monferrato"*, sweetened meatballs made with roasted veal and apples.

Trattoria Piemontese €€

Address: Via Napione, 45, 10124 Turin
Tel. 0039 011 812 2714. www.trattoriapiemontese.it
Opening hours: Tuesday – Saturday 7.30 – 11pm, Sunday 12 – 2.30pm, 7.30 – 11pm. Closed on Monday.

For more than 50 years, this simple trattoria has been offering excellent regional dishes. Like in any traditional trattoria, stick to local dishes and you won't be disappointed: *finanziera*, *tajarin* pasta, *cervella fritta* (yes, calf's brain fried in butter!), *bollito misto*, *brasato*. They also make good *fritto misto* but it has to be ordered at least two days in advance. It is served in three courses: fried vegetables, then meat and, to conclude, fried fruit and other sweet bits that, all combined, make a glorious hearty dish. Friendly energetic waiters speak some English.

06 HAZELNUT CAKE, ZABAIONE DESSERT AND PEPPERS WITH TUNA

Hello, my name is Veronica Geraci. I have lived in Turin all my life, except for a few years that I spent abroad studying and working. I manage the press office in the National Museum of Cinema here in Turin and, in my spare time, I teach cooking classes.

Favourite dishes: I am a big fan of the traditional Piedmontese cuisine. Among my favourites are *vitello tonnato*, *peperoni con il tonno*, *agnolotti del plin* (only those made by hand with a filling of three different types of meat), desserts such *torta di nocciole* and *zabaione*.

Vitello tonnato – see page 10.

Peperoni con il tonno – a traditional appetiser that is served cold. Strips of roasted peppers are topped with a mix of tuna, anchovies, capers and homemade mayonnaise. Some of the best peppers in the region, peperoni di Carmagnola, are grown in the province of Turin.

Agnolotti del plin – a type of traditional stuffed pasta originating in the areas of Langhe and Monferrato. Small in size, *agnolotti del plin* are always pinched on the sides (hence the name "plin" which in a local dialect means "pinch"). In old days, the filling was made with leftovers from the meat roast and varied from family to family. In the small town of Calliano in the Province of Asti, donkey meat is used for the stuffing. Nowadays, the purists say that real *agnolotti del plin* have to be made with a mix of roasted beef (or veal), pork and rabbit and served with the juices from the roast. However, most restaurants offer a single meat filling nowadays (see **Le Tre Galline** on page 64).

Torta di nocciole – a hazelnut cake originating from the Langhe area of Piedmont. The recipe varies widely and you will find that almost every bakery, café or restaurant in Turin have their own interpretation of this delicious traditional cake, however, the basic ingredients are flour, eggs, butter, sugar and *La Tonda Gentile* hazelnuts with the IGP (*Indicazione Geografica Protetta*) designation that guarantees quality. The best cakes are made with lightly toasted hazelnuts that are roughly ground afterwards. Traditionally, the *torta di nocciole* is accompanied by *zabaione* cream.

Zabaione (or zabajone) – a sweet thick beverage made with egg yolks, sugar, and Marsala wine, all whisked over a simmering water bath. The more traditional way is serving it warm in a glass and you might see some locals enjoying it with a buttery croissant for breakfast. Many restaurants also serve it as a dessert or sauce poured over fruit or cakes.

Why: These dishes represent Piedmont's identity and bring back my childhood memories. I remember when I was little my mother asked me to help her to make *vitello tonnato* and put the sauce on the meat. Needless to say, more sauce ended up in my stomach than on the plate.

Where: I like cooking and eating these dishes at home. When I have guests from other parts of Italy, they are always amazed by the variety and deliciousness of appetisers that we have in Piedmont. Many years ago it was possible to taste traditional dishes in *piole* (traditional osterias in Piedmont; for more see "Rub shoulders with locals in a traditional piola" on page 67) but nowadays almost all of them have disappeared. If you want to eat like locals I would suggest going to the historic areas of

Quadrilatero Romano and San Salvario that are cosmopolitan yet have managed to retain their identity. There you will often find a kebab place beside a traditional osteria. Try a degustation menu ("il menù degustazione") in the restaurant **Quanto Basta** to taste *vitello tonnato, peperoni con il tonno, agnolotti del plin* all at once. Sometimes I allow myself the luxury of buying *agnolotti* in the delicatessen Steffanone where everything is the highest quality. A good *torta di nocciole* can be found in the confectioner's Stratta that used to supply the royal house of Savoy. I get ecstatic over *spuma di zabaione* in **Quanto Basta** and *zabaione al Parmigiano Reggiano* in the restaurant **La Sartoria**.

QUANTO BASTA € €

Address: Via San Domenico 12-b, 10122 Turin
Tel. 0039 011 521 4452
Opening hours: Thursday – Tuesday, 12 – 3pm, 7.30 – 11pm.
Closed on Wednesday. www.quantobastaristorante.it
For more see page 47.

GASTRONOMIA STEFFANONE

Address: Via Maria Vittoria, 2, 10123 Turin
Opening hours: Tuesday – Saturday 8.30am – 3.30pm.
Closed on Sunday and Monday. www.steffanone.it
For more see the sidebar "Delicatessens that locals love" on page 55.

CONFETTERIA STRATTA

Address: Piazza San Carlo, 191, 10123 Turin. Opening hours: Tuesday – Saturday 9am – 7pm, Sunday 9.30am – 7pm.
Closed on Monday. www.stratta1836.it
For more see the sidebar "Adresses for chocolate lovers" on page 24.

La Sartoria Cucina su Misura € €

Address: Via Sant'Anselmo, 27/A, 10125 Turin
Tel. 0039 011 0461683
Opening hours: Monday 8pm – 11.30pm,
Tuesday – Saturday 1pm – 2pm, 8pm – 11.30pm.
Closed on Sunday. www.ristorantelasartoria.com

Here traditional recipes and ingredients are interpreted with a modern twist. You can choose between two dish sizes, medium or large, with the latter being certainly a better value. For tables of four people and more the menu is limited. Try the piglet cooked three ways *(Il Maialino in tre parti e in tre cotture)*, excellent risotto with Blu del Moncenisio cheese and seasonal appetisers. The restaurant is small and gets quite busy, so it is better to book or have a backup option.

Gastronomia Steffanone

DELICATESSENS THAT LOCALS LOVE

Turin, like many big Italian cities, has many delicatessens (*gastronomie*). I would describe these venerable shops as fancy take-aways as they sell prepared home-style foods, from appetisers to main courses and desserts. Visiting them is like stepping back in time as *gastronomie* are real custodians of Turin's culinary traditions. Their range of dishes and products rarely change no matter what gastronomic trends sweep the city. Here you will find an array of cured meats and cheeses, various types of pasta, lasagne, *vitello tonnato*, meats cooked and soaked in rich sauces, all sold by weight. Each residential area has at least one *gastronomia*, with some of the oldest and most famous located in the city centre. Stock up in one of these shops before heading to a picnic or if you have a kitchen in your holiday let. Some delicatessens have one or two tables, so you can have a quick lunch or dinner there. The prices are not low and, in some of the more celebrated historical shops, you might end up paying as much as a meal costs in a restaurant. Locals often place orders with their local *gastronomia* to cater for a special lunch, dinner or wedding reception.

Steffanone

Address: Via Maria Vittoria, 2, 10123 Turin
Opening hours: Tuesday – Saturday 8.30am – 3.30pm.
Closed on Sunday and Monday. www.steffanone.it

One of the oldest and most famous delicatessen in Turin, Steffanone opened in 1886. Its founder, Luigi, brought the most sophisticated European and regional dishes to the tables of wealthy locals. Apparently, the shop was the first one to start selling the *insalata russa* (a salad made with boiled potatoes, carrots, peas, pickles and eggs dressed in generous amounts of mayonnaise) in Italy in the early 1900s. Today, the *gastronomia* is renowned for such traditional dishes as *brasato al Barolo, agnolotti pasta,* and *finanziera*. Your purchases are wrapped in waxed logoed paper and the pack is tied with a piece of thick red cotton thread. You can sometimes see locals coming in with their own serving dishes, so the staff can

55

expertly arrange elaborate appetisers for them. Looking for something very decadent to try? Buy the fried and marinated eel (*anguilla in carpione*) priced at 100 euros per kilo.

Baudracco

Address: Corso Vittorio Emanuele II, 62, 10121 Turin
Opening hours: Tuesday – Saturday 9am-1pm, 3.30-7.30pm. Closed on Sunday and Monday.

A short stroll from the Porta Nuova train station, this spacious family-run shop is stuffed to the brim with delicacies many of which are displayed in the window: stuffed eggs, the ubiquitous *insalata russa*, traditional meat appetisers set in wobbly jelly, a huge range of traditional regional dishes, potato pies, different types of lasagne and pasta, various desserts, including the delicious *il bonet*. The delicatessen is famous for its cooked hams made on the premises and mousse of cotechino pork sausage sold in jars. They also have an excellent choice of cheeses from Piedmont's Alpine pastures (the Blu del Moncenisio and Raschera d'alpeggio that I bought were divine), decent range of wines and delicious preserves made with heritage fruit varieties.

Insalata russa

Rosada

Address: Via Magenta, 10, 10128 Turin
Opening hours: Tuesday – Saturday 8.30am – 1pm, 4 – 7.30pm.
Closed on Sunday and Monday. www.rosadadal1926.it

For three generations, since 1926, the Rosada family has been selling high quality prepared home-style foods. On any given day, you will find more than 40 different prepared dishes to take home. Try their *insalata russa* with seafood (the closest you can find to the original old recipe), liver pâté, *fricandò di carne* (traditional meat and potato stew) and the old-style *rotolo appetitoso* (egg roulade filled with mayonnaise and boiled ham). Apart from a small range of wines, they also sell excellent artisan beers.

La Cambusa del Bastimento

Address: Via Della Rocca, 6/E, 10123 Turin
Opening hours: Monday – Saturday 10.30am – 3pm, 6 – 8.30pm.
Closed on Sunday. www.lacambusadelbastimento.it

Despite what is often said about landlocked cities, Turin has some outstanding eateries for fish lovers. This recently open seafood delicatessen is a fine example. A small range of dishes are prepared daily in the open kitchen: stewed sea bass, octopus in wine, fish soups, seafood salads. They also sell jars with various seafood sauces, octopus preserved in oil, *acciughe al verde*, fish ragù, seafood salami and other delicacies. There is also a couple of tables where you can eat freshly made reasonably priced dishes.

My name is Ivana Sanfilippo. I was born in Turin and have lived in the city all my life. At the moment I am not working but I would like one day to run a small café with a flower shop, where I could indulge in my fantasies making delicious desserts that my customers would enjoy surrounded by plants and flowers.

Favourite dishes: the starters that I like are *tomini al verde, agnolotti al sugo d'arrosto* and *tagliatelle al sugo d'arrosto* is my favourite pasta dish, and, for sweet treats, I like *marrons glacés*. I would also like to mention *il marocchino* coffee drink that is delicious.

Tomini al verde – see page 10.

Agnolotti – a meat-filled pasta. Its shape varies depending on the area of the region. The filling is made with roasted or boiled veal and spinach. They can be served with a meat sauce (*al sugo d'arrosto*), in a broth or with sage, butter and parmesan.

Marrons glacés – candied chestnuts that are used for various desserts or eaten on their own. Chestnuts in sugar syrup have been enjoyed as a treat in Piedmont since the 15th century, however, the origins of the shiny *marrons glacés* recipe have been long disputed between Italians and the French. The latter say that the first written recipe of the delicacy hailed from the Versailles court in the 1600s. Italians claim that the cook of Charles Emmanuel I, Duke of Savoy, invented *marrons glacés* using the chestnuts from the Cuneo area.

Il marocchino – originating from the city of Alessandria in Piedmont in the 1990s, the drink is considered by purists more of a trendy variation of *bicerin* (see page 35) rather than coffee. *Marocchino* is served in a small glass, slightly bigger than an espresso cup. The glass is first dusted with cacao powder, hot milk foam is added, then coffee is poured and everything is topped with a sprinkle of cacao. Locals tend to drink *marocchino* mid-morning or in the afternoon.

Why: All these come from the old cooking traditions and I love their taste. If I have guests from outside of Turin, I cook these dishes for them at home.

Where: Most restaurants in the city have adapted traditional dishes to the modern palate. However, in trattorie in small towns and villages near Turin you can still find their original versions. *Il marocchino* can be found in almost any café or bar in the city.

Tip from a local: For an additional exquisite flavour, ask the barman to smear the bottom of the glass with Nutella when ordering Il Marocchino.

La Capanna Dei Nonni €

Address: Via Sebastiano Caboto, 42, 10129 Turin
Tel. 0039 011 505424
Opening hours: Monday – Saturday 10.15am – 7.30pm.
Closed on Sunday.

A small deli-style eatery with a great selection of fresh pasta dishes including *agnolotti*. Although it is not centrally located, it fills up quickly and if you turn up without a reservation, you might have to be patient and wait for a table. Please note: it is only open for lunch.

Pasticceria Sacco

Address: Corso De Gasperi, 9, 10129 Turin
Opening hours: Tuesday – Saturday 8am – 7.30pm,
Sunday 8am – 1pm. www.saccopasticceriatorino.it

Open since 1956. With the workshop located above the retail space, the delicacies on sale are always fresh. Excellent quality *marrons glacés* are made strictly by hand on the premises and sold during autumn and winter. There is a small café where you can sample the baked goodies.

Marrons glacés

GASTRONOMIC EVENTS IN TURIN

Turin's residents love gastronomic events and there are many to choose from all year round in the city and nearby towns. Some of them attract international foodies with many activities in English, others only Italian gourmands. In summer, you are likely to stumble across small local events, pop-up farmers' markets and street food festivals.

CioccolaTò

Since November 2004, the city hosts the CioccolaTò festival with over 100 international and Italian chocolate makers setting up stands in Piazza San Carlo. Here you will find big commercial and smaller confectionery brands as well as fair trade and vegan chocolate makers. During the festival many restaurants, bars and cafes in the city centre offer chocolate themed menus. Although all tastings, baking demonstrations, cultural events and workshops are in Italian, you don't need to speak the language to enjoy many free samples given by the vendors and all kinds of chocolate sold by the kilo.
www.cioccola-to.it

Passione Cioccolato

If you prefer high quality artisan chocolate you will enjoy this festival more than CioccolaTò. A small number of chocolatiers from Turin and Piedmont demonstrate their delectable creations, give master classes and cooking demonstrations in the beautiful surroundings of the Medieval Hamlet (Borgo Medievale) in the Parco Valentino. The first edition of the festival in April of 2015 proved a great success with thousands of Torinesi turning up despite torrential rains. The small squares and porticoes of the hamlet were taken up by artisans selling exquisite hazelnuts from the Le Langhe area, various desserts, excellent gelato and other delicacies from the region and across Italy. Foodies also enjoyed guided chocolate tastings, cooking demonstrations and classes on matching chocolate with beer and vermouth.
www.passionecioccolato.it

Terra Madre Salone del Gusto

This is an important international food event that brings together the city residents, tourists, Slow Food activists and delegates from 160 countries around the world. The festival spreads around the city: tastings, workshops, cooking demonstrations take place in parks, museums, historical buildings and various neighbourhoods. Via Po, with its arcades and old historic cafes, turns into the Via del Gelato (Ice Cream Street) hosting tastings, meetings with producers and a large laboratory inside Alberto Marchetti's ice cream shop. You can go on a tour of Porta Palazzo, Europe's largest open-air market or hire a personal food shopper to navigate the Slow Food market in Parco Valentino with vendors from five continents. Many events are in English. To see the full programme go to the festival's website.
www.salonedelgusto.com/en

International Festival of *Bagnet Verd*

Locals in Turin love their *bagnet verd*, a strong green sauce made with parsley, garlic, olive oil, vinegar, anchovies and bread crumbs, which they put on meat, *tomini* cheeses and numerous appetisers (*tomini al verde* – see page 10, *acciughe al verde* – see page 75). For several years, local business owners in the vibrant San Salvario neighbourhood have been organising the International Festival of *Bagnet Verd* on Piazza Madama Cristina. 50 teams, chefs and amateurs alike, compete by chopping up the simple ingredients and letting the spectators choose the best sauce. There is also a young designers market, live music and, in the evening, a feast in the piazza (booking is essential) where local eateries serve traditional dishes with, naturally, *bagnet verd*.
www.bagnettoverde.it

Birra D'Ecc Festival

More than a dozen Italian small breweries get together for this open-air festival to ply thirsty locals with excellent craft beers. DJs, live bands playing everything from blues to rock and many stands selling delicious Italian and international street food make this noisy festival a great way to mingle with Turin residents. Check the festival's website for the location and dates as they can vary.
www.birradecc.it

08 VEGETABLES IN TOMATO SAUCE, MEAT RAVIOLI AND COCOA PUDDING

My name is Benedetta Oggero, I was born and raised in Turin and currently work as an English teacher. I am passionate about cooking and love hosting social eating events through Gnammo.com.

Favourite dishes: I love *antipasto Piemontese*, which you can eat as an appetiser adding some tuna to it to make it more filling. As for the pasta, I adore *agnolotti del plin*, tiny *ravioli*; the best ones have a perfect balance between stuffing and the dough. My favourite dessert is *bonet*, a chocolate pudding served cold.

Antipasto Piemontese, or *giardiniera Piemontese* - vegetables preserved in a tomato sauce. Traditionally the preserve is made at the end of the summer with ripe tomatoes, green beans, carrots, bell peppers, onions, cauliflower and wine vinegar. Served cold with tuna, bread or breadsticks.

Agnolotti del plin – see page 51.

Bonet (or *bunet*) – a rich pudding made with milk, eggs, cocoa powder, rum and amaretti biscuits cooked over a simmering water bath. In the Langhe area, hazelnuts can also be added to the mix. It is served cold. First mention of the dessert dates back to the 13th century when it was served during feasts in noble families. The early recipes didn't include chocolate as it was added some centuries later. "*Il bonet alla monferrina*", the ancient chocolate-free pudding is very difficult to find nowadays.

Why: I love these dishes as they remind me of my childhood, special dinner parties, people who are not here any longer. *Agnolotti del plin* are special to me because in my family we always eat them for Christmas or other family festivities. My grandmother was a great cook and put *agnolotti* on the table only for special occasions as they are difficult and time-consuming to make.

Where: I enjoy eating them in typical restaurants here in Turin but the best ones are served at traditional trattorias, *piole*, in the countryside.

Antica trattoria delle Langhe €

Address: Via Luigi Capriolo, 45, 10139 Turin
Tel. 0039 011 3824214
Opening hours: Wednesday – Sunday, 12pm – 2pm, 7.30pm – 10pm, Tuesday 7.30pm – 10pm. Closed on Monday.
This family-run restaurant serves typical dishes from the Langhe area of Piedmont. The décor makes you think more of an Italian nonna's sitting room than a trattoria. The dishes are simple, just like in older times. Try the *tagliolini alla bagna cauda* pasta, *agnolotti* and *carbonata* meat stew for an extra-hearty traditional meal. Call to book a table on weekends.

Le Tre Galline € € €

Address: Via Gian Francesco Bellezia, 37, 10122 Turin
Tel. 0039 011 4366553
Opening hours: Monday – Friday 7.30pm – 10.15pm,
Saturday 12.30pm – 2.15pm, 7.30pm – 10.15pm,
Sunday 12.30pm – 2.15pm. www.3galline.it
This small restaurant is renowned for their legendary *agnolotti*

ai tre arrosti (made with three different types of meat, just like in the old days) and *bollito misto* (slowly cooked beef mixed with less noble bits such as tail and cotechino as well as pieces of boiled capon and pork). The *bollito* is sliced in front of you on a trolley and served with a range of delicious sauces. Try their degustation menu for 50 euros to enjoy such typical local dishes as *vitello tonnato, carne cruda, insalata russa, agnolotti torinesi al sugo d'arrosto* and *bunet* in one sitting.

Favourite ice cream shops: In L'Essenza del Gelato, in addition to the classic flavours, they use seasonal ingredients. I am still dreaming about their persimmon ice cream paired with a *marron glace* flavour which I had last autumn!

Tip from a Local: Visit Turin in winter to enjoy rich local dishes that might feel too heavy in summer.

Gelateria L'Essenza del Gelato

Address: Via Principe Amedeo, 21F, 10123 Turin
Opening hours: Monday - Wednesday 12pm – 8pm,
Thursday – Sunday 12pm – 11pm. Might be closed on rainy days!
www.essenzadelgelato.it

This small artisan gelateria goes easy on sugar, doesn't use any colourants, preservatives or other chemical nasties. In winter, they also make rich decadent hot chocolate. Flavours change with seasons. I liked the *Principe Amadeo* flavour, a dark chocolate and hazelnut gelato with a touch of salt as well as *ricotta fichi e mandorla*.

New food trends in the city: We have a lot of new sushi and Japanese cuisine restaurants as this is what is cool at the moment. I adore sushi and Japanese food in general, so I am really enjoying the trend! I really like **Daiichi** that offer elegant and delicious sushi and also thai food. **Ichi** has an all-you-can-eat formula without compromising on quality.

Daiichi Sushi € €

Address: Via IV Marzo, 5, 10122 Turin

Tel. 0039 011 0193400

Opening hours: Monday – Friday, 12.30pm – 2.30pm, 7.30pm – 12am, Saturday 7.30pm – 12am. Closed on Sunday.

www.daiichi.it.

You will see Japanese and Thai dishes on the menu here. It is packed with locals on weekends, so make sure to reserve a table. Desserts are a mix of local gelato from **Di Fiorio**, *sorbetto* and oriental concoctions such as red bean paste with coconut milk and green tea.

Ichi Sushi € €

Address: Corso Unione Sovietica, 355, 10135 Turin

Tel. 0039 011 19504923

Opening hours: Monday – Friday, 12pm – 3pm, 7pm – 11.45pm.

www.ristorantegiapponeseichi.it

Locals love this restaurant's all-you-can-eat formula for lunch as well as dinner. The evening menu offers more variety.

RUB SHOULDERS WITH LOCALS IN A TRADITIONAL PIOLA

You will not hear the word *"piola"* (*piole* plural) outside of Piedmont. It means a small traditional eatery where inexpensive simple meals are served. In old days, it was somewhat of a mix between a bar and osteria where locals came to have a glass of wine, have a simple meal, sing and gossip. Nowadays, *piole* are slowly disappearing giving way to modern sleek restaurants with more elaborate menus and wine lists. However, a few real unrefined and honest *piola* eateries, often run by older generation locals, still survive in the city. Do not expect a menu in English or any menu at all. In many *piole* you will see a blackboard with the few dishes that are offered or you will be told what is available on the day. Do not let that put you off, just ask for a starter *(antipasto)*, pasta dish *(primo)* and/or main meat dish *(secondo)* and enjoy the hearty local fare. Some old *piole* are open all day but hot food is served only during lunch and dinner hours while drinks with light snacks (cured meats, cheese boards, panini sandwiches) can be ordered throughout the day. Make sure you have enough cash in your wallet, as many of them do not accept credit cards.

Caffè Vini Emilio Ranzini €

Address: Via Porta Palatina, 9, 10122 Turin
Tel. 0039 011 765 0477
Opening hours: Monday – Friday 9.30 am – 8.30pm,
Saturday 10.30am – 5pm. Closed on Sunday.

Entering this small unassuming family-run *piola* is like stepping back in time. Open since the 1950s, it serves cold meals in style of *"la merenda sinoira"* (see page 11): *acciughe al verde, vitello tonnato, uova soda* (yes, hard-boiled eggs are served here, just like in good old days!), *antipasto piemontese*. Ask for a *tagliere*, a mix of sliced local cheeses and cured meats, if you want to taste such delicacies as *la mocetta*, an artisan salami made using an ancient method high in the Alps, artisan *salsiccia cruda, blu di Lanzo* and *gorgonzola* cheeses. In summer, you can sit in the tiny courtyard (if you are lucky to find space!). Be warned, it is packed with friendly local drunkards, professionals, students, artists and occasional tourists for lunch and dinner.

Piola Da Celso €

Address: Via Verzuolo, 40, 10139 Turin
Tel. 0039 011 4331202
Opening hours: Monday – Wednesday 7.30am – 9pm,
Thursday – Saturday 8am – 12am. Closed on Sunday.

Located in what once was a workmen's neighbourhood, Borgo San Paolo, this small *piola* has not changed for decades. The owner, energetic 80-something year-old Celso, greets clients and chats with some in a Piedmontese dialect. Here you will find all traditional fare: *acciughe al verde*, old style *vitello tonnato*, *peperoni con la bagna caoda*, *bollito*, excellent *agnolotti*. On weekends, it gets very busy and you might have to wait to be served. Book your table in advance for dinner on Thursday, Friday and Saturday.

Da Cianci Piola Caffé €

Address: Largo IV Marzo, 9/b, 10122 Turin
Tel. 0039 388 876 7003
Opening hours: Every day, 12.45 – 3.30pm, 6.30 – 11pm.

A few steps from the main Piazza Castello, this place has an unbeatable reputation for excellent food and good value. The menu here is short and offers only a few dishes that change often and are always seasonal and delicious. Excellent *carne cruda* and *tomini* are served as appetisers. Order an *antipasto misto* if you want to taste different appetisers at once. It has become so popular lately that getting a table for dinner is almost impossible (they rarely answer the phone but try calling at least a day in advance). To avoid disappointment head there for lunch but make sure you arrive 10-15 minutes before the opening time. You can admire the pretty square where the *piola* is located while waiting.

09 40-YOLKS PASTA, BRAISED MEAT AND DELICIOUS ICE CREAM INVENTED BY THE FAMILY

 My name is Edoardo Cavagnino and I have been living in Turin for 30 years. Since 2007 I have been working for my family's business, Gelati Pepino 1884, the oldest ice cream maker in Europe. I am the President of the company.

Favourite dishes: *carne cruda di Fassone battuta al coltello* served with marinated vegetables and *tomini* cheeses, *tajarin ai 40 tuorli* with white Alba truffle, *brasato al Barolo*, and, naturally, one of our ice creams, *Pinguino alla crema*.

Carne cruda di Fassone battuta al coltello – see page 28.
Tajarin ai 40 tuorli – see page 35.
Brasato al Barolo – beef braised in Barolo wine, a classic Piemontese dish. The beef is marinated in wine for 24 hours before it is cooked slowly. Nowadays, the expensive Barolo is often replaced with other good but cheaper red wines, such as Barbera Dolcetto or Gattinara. One or two thick slices of brasato are normally served with polenta or boiled potatoes.
Pinguino alla crema – the classic cream flavour of the world's first chocolate-covered ice cream on a stick invented in 1939. For more see page 46.

Why: I love these dishes because some of them connect me with the past and history of my family. Ice cream has always been part of my life given the family's business. When I brought it for

69

everyone in my class at school, it was a day of celebrations! As I was growing up my father brought me with him to see antique markets and we would always have a break to eat some *tomini* cheese and salami. The simplicity and centuries-old tradition of *tomini* and *tajarin* pasta have always fascinated me.

Tip from a Local: Do not try to find tajarin pasta with white truffles in summer. It is a seasonal dish served only in winter.

Where: I have always been curious about food, which pushes me to try new things, but for classic flavours, you have to go to the right places. To eat traditional dishes like a real Torinese there is no other option but going to an old style eatery called "*piola*" or typical trattoria, which you can find in the historic district of Borgo Dora and Quadrilatero Romano. Those places are ageless!

Da Cianci Piola Caffé €

Address: Largo IV Marzo, 9/b, 10122 Turin.
Tel. 0039 388 876 7003
Opening hours: Every day, 12.45pm – 3.30pm, 6.30pm – 11pm
This small centrally located place fills up quickly, so arrive early or book in advance. The menu is short and offers only a few dishes that are always seasonal and delicious. For more see "Rub shoulders with locals in a traditional *piola*" on page 67.

I Valenza € €

Address: via Borgo Dora 39, 10152 Turin.

Tel. 0039 011 521 3914

Opening hours: Tuesday – Saturday, 12pm – 3.30pm, 8pm – 11pm. Closed on Sunday and Monday.

Located in a residential area near the historic antique market Balon, this family-run trattoria is a hit with locals. The décor has not changed much since the 1970s and the menu is only in Italian but, whatever you pick, you are guaranteed to get great homemade regional food. The owner Walter can come across as cranky and smokes inside sometimes but locals love the place for its old-timey atmosphere. In the evening, there is often traditional live music with the owner and customers singing along. Try their exceptionally good *tajarin* pasta.

Tip from a local: The trattoria is also open every second Sunday of the month when the large flea market Gran Balon takes place in the area. Book in advance!

Al Monferrato € € €

Address: Via Monferrato 6, 10131 Turin

Tel. 0039 011 819 0661

Opening hours: Monday – Saturday, 12.30pm – 2.30pm, 7.45pm – 10.30pm. Closed on Sunday. www.ristorantemonferrato.com.

This elegant restaurant has been serving classical Torinese cuisine since 1820. The menu is seasonal with a focus on typical meat of the regional Piedmontese Fassone and Bue Grasso di Carru' breeds. Edoardo says they make excellent *tajarin* pasta.

La Baita dal Formagg

Address: Via Lagrange, 36, 10123 Turin

Tel. 0039 011 5623224

Opening hours: Monday – Saturday, 8.30am-1pm, 3.30pm-7.30pm. Closed on Sunday.

This cheese shop has been delighting locals since 1963 with excellent cheeses, charcuterie, preserves and many delectable local specialties. Edoardo recommends trying their *tomini* and artisan goat cheese as well as other raw milk cheeses made on the Alpine pastures in Piedmont. For more see "Addresses for cheese lovers" on page 79).

Favourite places for breakfast: a traditional Torino breakfast calls for a *bicerin* or hot *zabaione*. However, nowadays, you will see locals taking a glass of freshly squeezed orange juice and *tramezzino* (a small sandwich) in a bar or coffee and croissant. I like having breakfast in our family's historic **Pepino Café** or **Samambaia Café**, both centrally located.

SANDWICH WITH STYLE

Do you think there is nothing sophisticated about a sandwich? Think again! The historic **Caffè Mulassano** does sandwiches like no other place in Turin. This is where the famous *tramezzino*, a soft sandwich with various fillings, was invented in 1926 and has been served with style ever since. You can choose from 30 classic, traditional and gourmet flavours such as chicken salad, tuna, *insalata russa*, *bagna cauda*, anchovies with butter, lobster, porcini mushrooms or truffles. Uniformed waiters bring the *tramezzini* on a silver serving stand to your table. The splendid surroundings with a small fountain, Italian Liberty style shiny brass, dark wood, polished marble, mirrors and frescoed ceilings guarantee the most refined sandwich experience of your life. Try the vermouth Mulassano, the aromatic drink made in the café's own distillery. Each drink comes with a plate of tiny *tramezzini* and costs 7-10 euros.

Caffè Mulassano
Address: Piazza Castello 15, 10100 Turin
Tel. 0039 011547990
Opening hours: Thursday – Tuesday 7.30am – 12am.
Closed on Wednesday. www.caffemulassano.com

Samambaia Café

Address: Via Madama Cristina 20, 10125 Turin
Opening hours: Monday – Saturday 7am – 7pm.
Closed on Sunday.

One of the most popular stops for breakfast and lunch in the San Salvario neighbourhood, this small coffee shop has been open for almost 100 years. The dark wood shelves are stoked with colourful tins and boxes of biscuits, jars of pickles and jams. The walls are covered in vintage posters and postcards. If you want to linger and relax over a cup of coffee, make sure you come here after breakfast and lunch hours as the place gets jam-packed with hungry locals.

Favourite place for lunch: In summer, there is nothing better than a walk in the Valentino park, along the River Po. In the park, there are several local rowing clubs. My favourite club is **Società Canottieri Cerea** (Viale Virgilio, 61) beside which is a small bar-restaurant with a terrace overlooking the river. There you can have an excellent lunch in summer.

Favourite ice cream shops: Naturally, our family-run Bar Café Pepino!

BAR CAFÉ PEPINO

Address: Piazza Carignano, 8, 10123 Turin

Opening hours: Tuesday – Thursday 9.30am – 10.30pm, Friday – Saturday 9.30am – 11.30pm, Sunday – Monday 9.30am – 9.30pm.

Edoardo's favourite ice creams are *Pinguino alla crema*, which reminds him of his childhood, as well as *crema Pepino* and *cacao fondente*. For more see page 48.

Gelateria Pepino

10 ANCHOVIES IN A GREEN SAUCE, LOCAL CHEESES AND HAZELNUT-CHOCOLATE SPREAD

My name is Alberto Bonis. I was born in Turin but when I was little, I lived all over Italy and Europe with my father for his work. I graduated from the Academi of Fine Arts in Turin and work as a graphic and web designer and illustrator. My work in the industrial field has taken me to the Middle East and Mexico.

Favourite dishes: I like typical regional dishes that often require collaborative preparation with participation of the whole family or fellow diners. My favourites are *acciughe al verde, ravioli del plin, bagna cauda* and *crema Gianduja*. I also adore all local cheeses, especially, *Gorgonzola* and *Castelmagno*.

Acciughe al verde – an appetiser consisting of salted anchovies marinated in a green sauce made with parsley, garlic, breadcrumbs, vinegar and olive oil. It is served cold, often as part of the *marenda sinoira* (see "La marenda sinoira" on page 11).
Ravioli del plin (also called *agnolotti* del plin) – see page 51.
Bagna cauda - see page 11.
Crema Gianduja – a sweet spread made with chocolate and roasted hazelnut paste. Only hazelnuts from Piedmont, that grow in the hills of the Langhe and Monferrato areas and have the IGP designation are used. Each confectioner in Turin has an original recipe that is often kept secret. The origins of *crema Gianduja*, like that of the classic chocolate *gianduiotto* (see page 18), can

be traced back to the 19th century when the British blockaded the Mediterranean and Turin suffered a shortage of cocoa. Locals generously spread *crema Gianduja* on bread for breakfast or use it for making cakes and pastries.

Gorgonzola – blue cheese produced from full fat cow's milk. For centuries, it was mainly made in the Lombardy region, however, over the last century Piedmont has become one of the leaders in *gorgonzola* production. There are two types of *gorgonzola*: *dolce* and *piccante*. *Gorgonzola dolce* is soft and creamy with a delicate taste; *gorgonzola piccante* is firmer, sometimes crumbly, and has a stronger, slightly peppery, flavour. Good quality soft *gorgonzola* is not cut in slices but scooped from the cheese wheel.

Castelmagno – one of Piedmont's most esteemed cheeses. With its origins dating back to the 13th century, it is one of Italy's oldest cheeses. *Castelmagno* is made with pasteurized cow's milk, with small amounts of goat's and sheep's milk added sometimes. Produced in only three small areas in the Cuneo province, the cheese has a D.O.P. designation. Sometimes it can have blue veins. Locals serve it in chunks with honey, use it in pasta dishes, risotto or for a ravioli filling. Real connoisseurs pair younger *Castelmagno* with Nebbiolo red wine while older blue-veined cheese can go well with Barolo.

Why: All these dishes have strong distinctive flavours; they are not "domesticated" or modernised but have their own particular character and a kind of hubris. They make me think of the past, when all food was made at home and cooking together was a ritual. Grandmothers prepared *ravioli del plin* and family gatherings were filled with discussions about better ways of cooking meat for making pasta fillings. The smell and taste of *bagna cauda* are strong and it is always eaten with a company, which creates somewhat of a goliardic camaraderie between the cooks and fellow diners that share a culinary experience that has peasant origins but has become somewhat elitist today.

Where: I like messing in the kitchen cooking for friends, for me a perfect lunch or dinner is always made at home. However, the centre of Turin is full of small restaurants with a cosy family atmosphere and exploring new places in search of another "home" is always exciting. **Cantine Barbaroux**, a few steps from Il Duomo, is my latest find of that kind and is worth another visit. I have a sweet tooth and going around small confectionery shops and pasticcerie to explore their artisan-made *crema Gianduja* is an adventure for me. My favourite is **Enodolceria di Servetto** where you can find all specialties of Piedmont, sweet and savoury. There are many cheese vendors at the **Porta Palazzo** market, who often offer great deals.

Cantine Barbaroux € €

Address: Via Giuseppe Barbaroux, 13, 10122 Turin
Tel. 0039 011 535412
Opening hours: Tuesday – Saturday 12pm-3pm, 7pm – 12am. Closed on Sunday and Monday.
Serving traditional regional dishes since 1902, this simple osteria is always full with locals at lunchtime. Set menus are good value although the service might not always be the friendliest. If you want to taste typical Piedmont's cured meats and cheeses order the appetisers *Salumi tipici* piemontesi and *Formaggi tipici piemontesi* that are good without fail.

Enodolceria di Servetto

Address: Piazza Statuto, 14, 10122 Turin

Opening hours: Tuesday – Saturday 9am – 1pm, 3pm – 7.30pm;
Monday 3pm – 7.30pm. Closed on Sunday.

www.enodolceriaservetto.it

A small delightful confectionary store filled to the brim with artisan chocolates, sweets, nougat, biscuits, honey, jams and other delicacies from across Italy and beyond. They also sell an excellent chocolate liquor, *crema Gianduja* chocolate spread, *grappa*, and more than 100 varieties of tea. A great place if you want to buy many edible gifts in one go. Everything can be gift wrapped.

Castelmagno cheese

ADDRESSES FOR CHEESE LOVERS

Piedmont, with its lush Alpine pastures, produces some of the best Italian cheeses, which are often called "the white gold" of the region. Cheese connoisseurs will love Turin's cheesemongers that sell everything, from famous D.O.P. ("protected designation of origin" in Italian) to rare cheeses produced by a handful of artisans. Don't be shy, ask for advice and the knowledgeable staff will be happy to help you as, in most cases, somebody in the shop speaks English. If you are after unusual local cheeses make sure to look for *Castelmagno d'alpeggio, cevrin di Coazze, saras del fen, sola* or *macagno* that are produced by artisans and can only be found in Piedmont. Most shops will vacuum-pack ("mettere sotto vuoto" in Italian) your cheese, just ask.

La Baita dël Fôrmagg

Address: Via Lagrange, 36, 10123 Turin.
Opening hours: Monday – Saturday 9am – 1pm, 4 – 7.30pm. Closed on Sunday.

This wonderful shop offers over 160 international, Italian and regional cheeses from renowned and small producers. Raw goat's milk cheeses from Alpine pastures near Turin, tiny *tomini di capra* with herbs and spices, *robiola di Roccaverano*, *toma d'Alba*, Castelmagno D.O.P., jars of *bruss* with *grappa*. Your purchases are wrapped in shiny waxed paper and tied with a piece of old-fashioned red cotton string. There is also a small range of fine wines, cured meats, jams and condiments to go with the cheeses you buy.

Làit e Formagg

Address: Via Madama Cristina, 18, 10125 Turin
Opening hours: Monday 11am – 2pm, 4 – 8pm;
Tuesday – Saturday 8am – 2pm, 4 – 8pm. Closed on Sunday.
www.alformaggi.it

Located in the heart of the lively San Salvario district, the shop sells a bit of everything: fresh pasta, gelato, yogurts, hazelnut cakes, quality cured meats such as *salsiccia di Bra* and *salame cotto* but their main focus is on carefully selected regional cheeses. Do not miss the *saras del fen*, a rare Alpine ricotta variety matured in hay and *murianengo* blue cheese which origins go back to the 11th century.

Borgiattino Formaggi i Vini

Address: Corso Vinzaglio, 29, 10121 Turin

Opening hours: Monday – Saturday 8.30am – 1pm, 4 – 7.30pm.

Closed on Wednesday and Sunday. www.borgiattino.com

The shop's focus is Italian and regional cheeses and there are many to choose from: the highly-prized *bettelmatt, murazzano D.O.P., macagno,* many raw milk goat's cheeses from the Alps. Ask for advice choosing wine, honey or jelly to match. A chunk of rare Piemontese cheese with a jar of jasmine or thyme jelly make an excellent gift for a foodie back home!

Mercato Metropolitano

Address: Piazza XVIII Dicembre, 4, 10122 Turin

Opening hours: Monday – Thursday 7.30am – 10.30pm, Friday – Saturday 7.30am – 12am, Sunday 7.30am – 10.30pm. www.mercatometropolitano.it

Located in the old Porta Susa train station this urban market is a great place to sample artisan beer, fresh pizza, have a quick meal or relax over a glass of organic prosecco. If you want to enjoy some local cheeses on the spot rather than bring them home, there is the L'Agricola cheese bar that sells *tagliere* (cheese board) priced from 6 to 18 euros, grilled raw milk goat's *tomini, robiola D'Alba* with truffles, *robiola di Roccaverano*. At lunch time, every Sunday there is live music to accompany your munching.

11 STUFFED PEACHES, CHICKPEA PANCAKES AND THE BEST CITY MARKETS

I am Alessandra Mazzotta. I have been living in Turin for 15 years working in environmental communications, writing for digital magazines, running a blog about green living www.ecoavoi.it and managing Verdessenza ecobottega (www.verdessenza.wordpress.com), a shop that sells fair trade, environmentally friendly products. I have written an e-book about food waste with practical tips on how to reduce it.

Favourite dishes: One of my favourite local dishes is delicious *acciughe al verde*, a tasty appetiser made with anchovies. You might ask how anchovies can be part of the traditional cuisine of Piedmont if there is no sea here in sight, not even if you look with binoculars. Anchovies, which are featured in many traditional regional dishes of Piedmont came from Liguria. They could be easily preserved in salt for long periods. Another dish that I adore is *la farinata*, originated in Genoa, Liguria, but is widely available in Turin. The desserts that I can never resist are il *bonet* and *pesche ripiene*.

Acciughe al verde – see page 75.
La farinata – an unleavened thin pancake that came to the city from Liguria. Historically, Turin has always had a strong trade connection with the port city of Genoa, so many Ligurian ingredients and dishes have been adopted in the city's cuisine. *La farinata* is made with simple ingredients: chickpea flour, water,

olive oil and salt, sometimes flavoured with rosemary and baked in a wood-fired oven. It has become one of the most popular street foods in Turin.

Pesche ripiene – see page 18.

Bonet – see page 63.

Why: I like these dishes because they are tasty, quick and simple to prepare. *La farinata* to me means a party with friends, a snack before or after going to the cinema that is perfect to eat hot while walking. It is irresistible! *Pesche ripiene* I like because of the taste combinations: the sweetness of the peaches, bitterness of the dark chocolate and amaretti biscuits. They are original in their simplicity, a great balance between healthy and naughty. An absolute must!

Where: Usually I eat these dishes in typical trattorias, old-style osterias that scrupulously preserve small variations of original recipes making them unique. *Acciughe al verde* are good at **Caffè della Basilica** and **Caffe-Vini Emilio Ranzini** (be warned, it is always full! For more see page 67). The best *farinata*, tasty and crispy as it should be, can be found in the small retro-style **pizzeria Da Gino**. Excellent *pesche ripiene*, when in season, are served in the restaurant **L'Acino** (see page 19) and trattoria **I Valenza**. I like the dessert *il bonet* in the modern **Il Camaleonte piola**. For a more formal dinner, I go to **Magorabin** or **Welcome Cargo Restaurant**.

Caffè della Basilica €€

Address: Via Della Basilica, 3/B, 10122 Turin
Tel. 0039 339 5061264, 0039 349 3549553
Opening hours: Monday – Saturday 12pm-2.30pm, 7.30pm – 2am.
Closed on Sunday. www.caffedellabasilica.it
A centrally located cosy wine bar with a simple décor that also

serves traditional dishes. The menu is short but updated on a regular basis and includes appetisers, pasta and meat, salads and desserts. Excellent choice of regional wines and artisan beers. Live jazz and blues concerts in the evening.

Pizzeria Da Gino €

Address: Via Monginevro, 46, 10141 Torino
Tel. 0039 011 3854335
Opening hours: Thursday – Tuesday 12pm – 2pm, 7pm – 11pm. Closed on Wednesday. www.ginopizzeria.it
This small pizzeria is always packed, especially in the evening, so come for lunch or arrive early if you don't want to queue. A choice of pizza slices is limited but of excellent quality. One of the best places in Turin for *farinata*. You can have a sit-down meal or order a take-away.

Trattoria I Valenza €

Address: Via Borgo Dora, 39, 10152 Turin
Tel. 0039 011 521 3914
Opening hours: Tuesday – Saturday 12 – 3.30pm, 7.30 – 10pm.
Alessandra says that the *pesche ripiene* dessert here is not to be missed (when in season, late summer-early autumn). For more see page 70.

Il Camaleonte piola €

Address: Via Claudio Luigi Berthollet, 9, 10125 Turin
Tel. 0039 011 650 4115
Opening hours: Monday – Thursday 5pm-12am,
Friday – Saturday 12pm – 1am.
A small eatery with a warm friendly atmosphere. The menu is short offering simple regional and Italian dishes with a modern twist and local ingredients. Every Friday, the menu features seafood and fish dishes. Make sure to sample typical Piedmont

starters, the bread made on premises, their home-made liqueurs and, as Alessandra suggests, *il bonet* dessert if available. Can get busy at dinnertime, especially on weekends, so make sure you book or have a backup plan.

Magorabin €€€

Address: Corso S. Maurizio, 61, 10124 Turin.
Tel. 0039 011 812 6808
Opening hours: Tuesday – Saturday 12pm – 3pm, 7pm – 11pm; Monday 7pm – 11pm. Closed on Sunday. www.magorabin.com
Centrally located in a historic building, Magorabin is one of the city's top restaurants for fine dining. Chef Marcello Trentini reinterprets traditional dishes with a personal touch. You can spend as little or as much as you want: there are set menus for 20, 30, 70 euros going all the way up to 160 euros for the Chef's Table with 18 latest dishes (this one has to be booked in advance for everyone at the table). If you want to taste Trentini's interpretations of traditional dishes order the *Divagazione Sul Territorio* menu with four dishes and a dessert.

Welcome Cargo Restaurant €€€

Address: Via Principe Tommaso, 18A Bis, 10125 Turin
Tel. 0039 011 020 6929
Opening hours: Tuesday – Sunday 7pm – 1am. Closed on Monday.
www.wcargorestaurant.it
While the majority of eateries in Turin take pride in sourcing their ingredients locally, this restaurant is unashamedly international. With a focus on highly prized delicacies from all over the globe, its menu features caviar from the Siberian Lake Baikal, wild salmon from Alaska, blue prawns from New Caledonia, Kobe beef, oysters from Ireland, France and Portugal. Even the décor is

different from anything you see in the city, reminiscent of trendy restaurants in New York or London. However, the bill at the end of the meal will bring you back to Turin as, despite the exotic ingredients, the prices are rather affordable and you can manage to have an excellent meal for 50 euros per head.

Local market: To see the real local market, head to the farmers' market at Porta Palazzo where you will find excellent prices, quality and folklore. Here I buy fruit and vegetables from Lina, an elderly lady that was the protagonist in an Italian documentary filmed in the city. I love her strawberries, carrots and cucumbers. Another great stand is that of Gianni, a man of few words, who has the best wild greens, often mixed with edible flowers such as violets. There is also Marcello who sells excellent kiwi, apricots and the best apples in the entire market.

Farinata

FOOD GALORE AT THE PORTA PALAZZO MARKET

Address: Piazza della Repubblica, 10152 Turin

www.scopriportapalazzo.com

Opening hours: **Antica Tettoia dell'Orologio** is open on Tuesday – Friday 8am – 1pm, 4pm – 7pm; Saturday 7.30am – 7.30pm. Closed on Monday.

Opening hours: **Farmers market** is open on Monday – Friday 7am – 1pm; Saturday 7am – 7pm. Closed on Sunday.

The largest open-air market in Europe **Porta Palazzo** has hundreds of stalls selling fruit, vegetables, cured meats, cheeses, fish and meat as well as clothes and household items at bargain prices. You might want to consult a map to navigate the market's 51,000 m2 area. For regional and Italian delicacies head to the covered market located in the beautiful early 20th-century building of **Antica Tettoia dell'Orologio** with its 88 stalls. Locals come here to buy some of the best cheeses from Alpine pastures, delicacies such as horse meat steaks, rabbit from Carmagnola, donkey meat *salami,* wild boar sausages, ethnic foods and exotic spices. I couldn't resist chunky dark *grissini al segalo* (rye breadsticks) from **Profumi del Forno** (Stand 1, at the back of the market) and enjoyed crunching them while watching locals shop.

To sample the best, buy a few scoops of creamy *gorgonzola dolce* and *tomini* from Cesaretto Claudio (Stand 6), slices of *bresaola d'Ossola* (air-cured salted beef), *Crudo di Cuneo D.O.P.* ham from Saba Daniele (Stand 72) and a bottle of Dolcetto d'Alba from the Enoteca De Luca Carlo (Stand 60).

At the back of the building, in the **Tettoia dei Contadini**, is a farmers market where 100 vendors sell local and organic produce from their farmlands. Here you will even find Chinese farmers who grow exotic fruit and vegetables near Turin. There are no imported foods in this part of the market!

12 MINI PASTRIES OF THE KINGS, WILD STRAWBERRY ICE CREAM AND RELAXING BRUNCHES

 Adriana Delfino has lived in Turin all her life. She designs and produces her own line of clothes and accessories since 1988 but prefers to define her occupation as a seamstress rather than a fashion designer. Her creations can be found in Talen.TO (Corso Vittorio Emanuele II 26/c), in Bottega Reale Museum Supershop in the Castello di Racconigi or in her studio (Via Madama Cristina, 74, by appointment only).

Favourite dishes: I love various desserts of Piedmont: cakes with hazelnuts and dark chocolate, so called *"dolci al cucchiaio"* and, especially, *pasticcini mignon.*

Dolci al cucchiaio – a category that unites Italian soft desserts such as custards, puddings, mousse that are often served in a glass cup and eaten with a spoon as opposed to "dry" desserts such as some cakes and biscuits. In Piedmont, the most popular *dolce al cucchiaio* is *il bonet* chocolate pudding (see page 63).

Pasticcini mignon – mini pastries, often called "the King's pastries" as they were popular at the royal court of Savoy. There are many different types of mini pastries: bignole torinesi, chantilly, tartelette, torcetti etc. You can buy them by weight in bakeries while in cafes they are often priced individually.

Why: *Pasticcini mignon* remind me of my childhood when, every Sunday, my father brought a tray of them from a local bakery.

Where: I enjoy them at home or in many historic cafes in the city. In **Caffè Al Bicerin**, you can have the famous *bicerin* drink (see page 37) with delicious mini pastries. My favourite *pasticcini mignon* are with pistacchio cream and with fruit at the **Pasticceria Ciccia**, the pastry shop that I like for their dedication to quality and a wide range of pastries.

CAFFÈ AL BICERIN

Address: Piazza della Consolata, 5, 10122 Torino
Opening hours: 8.30am – 7.30pm, closed on Wednesday.
www.bicerin.it
For more see page 37.

PASTICCERIA CICCIA

Address: Via Vincenzo Monti, 18, 10126 Turin
Opening hours: Tuesday – Saturday 8am – 8pm,
Sunday 8am – 1.30pm. Closed on Monday.
Open since 1982, this family-run pastry shop is famous in the vibrant San Salvario neighbourhood. It is packed with locals every morning grabbing a quick cappuccino and freshly baked croissant. During Pope Francesco's visit to Turin in 2015, the pasticceria Ciccia made a chocolate and pear cake for one of his official lunches. The cake weighed almost seven kilos and, according to the local press, it was so good that not a crumble was left after the meal. On Sunday mornings, there is often a long queue of loyal customers outside the shop.

Favourite ice cream shops: In La Mara dei Boschi the ingredients are strictly local and seasonal, so the ice cream is of unparalleled quality. My favourite flavours are *la mara dei boschi* (a type of wild strawberry), *il fondente all'arancio* (dark chocolate with orange), white chocolate with lemon. Their whipped cream is superb!

La Mara dei Boschi

Address: Via Berthollet, 30, 10125 Turin

Opening hours: Tuesday – Thursday 1pm – 9pm,

Friday 1pm – 10pm, Saturday 12pm – 10pm, Sunday 12pm – 9pm.

Closed on Monday. www.maradeiboschi.it

Marco Serra, the owner, likes to call his shop an ice cream laboratory and it is certainly not your run-of-the-mill shop. You are likely to find some very unusual flavours such as salted orange, sorbetto with grappa or Barolo wine. During cold seasons, try their luscious vegan *Gianduia* hot chocolate. A branch of Mara Dei Boschi has recently opened in the town of Alba where you can taste a truffle ice cream.

New food trends in the city: Brunch is a new habit for Turin residents. The new trend has been welcomed with enthusiasm by 30-40-year-olds who, after having a lie-in, sort out in one go their breakfast and lunch on Saturday and Sunday mornings without having to cook. For an excellent brunch I would recommend **Circolo dei Lettori** where you will find pancakes, French toast, eggs&bacon, savoury tarts, cheese boards, a wide choice of cured meats and many other things.

Circolo dei Lettori €€

Address: Via Giambattista Bogino, 9, first floor, 10123 Turin (to buzz in enter the code 1115 followed by the bell button).

Tel. 0039 011 4326827

Opening hours: Monday – Saturday 9.30am – 10pm. Also open on Sundays during certain events. www.circololettori.it

A truly hidden gem, the café (it is called Barney's but locals refer to it as Circolo dei Lettori) is located in a magnificent 17th century Palazzo Graneri della Roccia. It is a public space entirely dedicated to reading supported by the Regional Department for Culture. Do not be intimidated by the grand opulent rooms, the atmosphere is warm, the staff is friendly and there is always someone at hand who speaks English. Brunch is served buffet style and costs 20 euros. For a full meal, go to the restaurant that serves excellent regional dishes for lunch and dinner. Booking is recommended.

Pasticcini mignon

BAKERIES THAT LOCALS LOVE

Residential areas of Turin have many old family-run bakeries frequented by a loyal clientele. In recent years, several new artisan bread shops opened in central locations becoming almost instant hits with locals who love their devotion to social causes, high-quality stone-milled flours and dedication to bread-making traditions. Many bakeries, apart from breads, sell *grissini* breadsticks, pizza slices, sweet pastries, cakes and often have a café at the back of the shop or a few tables outside where you can have a quick tasty breakfast or lunch.

Perino Vesco

Address: Via Cavour, 10, 10123 Turin
Opening hours: Monday – Saturday 7.30 – 19.30.
Closed on Sunday. www.perinovesco.it

Open since 2007, this excellent bakery has a loyal following and is almost always packed, so be patient. Andrea Perino and his wife Chiara Vesco with a team of expert helpers bake a wide range of delicious sourdough breads using only stone-milled, mostly organic flours. Their hand-stretched savoury and sweet *grissini* are divine and come in many different flavours (I loved the ones with olives and also couldn't resist *grissini al cioccolato*). Pizza, small *pizzette*, *focaccia*, pretzels, strudel, tarts, - the choice is overwhelming! At the back, there is a café where you can order a freshly made *panino* (there are 20 types on the menu made with seasonal ingredients) or gobble up a buttery croissant. If you fancy something sweet to take home, grab a *torta Langarola di nocciole*, heavenly hazelnut cake, one of the best in the city.

Farina nel Sacco

Address: Via San Secondo 10/F, 10128 Turin
Opening hours: Monday – Friday 8am – 2pm, 4pm – 7.30pm; Saturday 8am – 1.30pm. Closed on Sunday. www.farinanelsacco.it
A short walk from Porta Nuova train station, this recently opened small bread shop is stocked with excellent sourdough breads made by prisoners training to be bakers in the local jail. The high quality flours, some of them are made from rare ancient grains, come from the oldest watermill in Piedmont. They also sell tasty pizza slices with classic and some unusual toppings (pizza with lard, walnuts and honey, anyone?), tarts, sweet and savoury *grissini*.

Panacea

Address: via San Massimo 5/bis, 10123 Turin
Opening hours: Monday – Saturday 8am – 8pm.
Closed on Sunday. www.panacea-torino.it
Managed by a social cooperative, the bakery prides itself on using flours from local grains cultivated in the fields of Stupinigi near Turin and only natural leavens. Its prices are

affordable. I tried their walnut, hemp and olive breads and loved them all. Bread at its best with a feel-good factor!

Panetteria Avetta

Adddress: Via Cibrario, 31 bis, 10143
Opening hours: Monday – Saturday 8am – 2pm, 4pm – 8pm. Closed on Sunday.

Since 1957, the Avetta family has been making quality breads in this traditional Turin-style bakery and many locals keep going back to refresh their childhood memories. The shop sells the classic range of breads, pizzas and fresh pastries. Some of their signature products include long-leavened *ciabatta* bread and *pane al malto* made with toasted malt and raisins (locals eat it for breakfast or with cured meats). To impress their customers, the bakery also makes *pane artistico*, buns shaped as flowers or figurines. In old days, every self-respecting bakery had those displayed in windows and they were sold for grand celebratory feasts. Very few bakeries in Turin make them nowadays.

ABOUT THE AUTHOR

Anna Lebedeva is a food and travel writer who has lived in Italy for over six years. She loves visiting small wineries and artisan producers, tasting traditional dishes wherever she goes and listening to nostalgic stories about days gone by that locals are always happy to share with her.

Did you like the book? Bite-sized foodie guides to other major Italian cities are coming out very soon.
Go to www.italywithgusto.com/books to sign up for new books alerts or email anna@italywithgusto.com

PHOTO CREDITS:

Front cover (left to right): ©rh2010/Adobe Stock, ©mc81 /Adobe Stock, ©zm_photo/Adobe Stock; page 15: ©Printemps/Adobe Stock; page 23: ©Anna Lebedeva; page 27: ©andraphoto58/Adobe Stock; page 31: ©Manuela Albertelli; page 33: ©menfis/Adobe Stock; page 38: ©Fassoneria Torino; page 44: ©Anna Lebedeva; page 54: ©Gastronomia Steffanone; page 56: ©Comugnero Silvana/Adobe Stock; page 60: ©helenedevun/Adobe Stock; page 74: ©Gelati Pepino; page 78: ©Claudio Baldini/Adobe Stock; page 85: ©Quanthem/Adobe Stock; page 90: ©makis7/Adobe Stock; back cover: (from left clockwise) ©mgoggio/Adobe Stock, ©vpardi/Adobe Stock, ©armando valente/Adobe Stock, ©Gelati Pepino.